That's My Bellybutton

That's My Bellybutton

Memoirs of a Pediatrician

Neil G. Aronson

To order additional copies of this book, contact:
Xlibris Corporation
1-888-795-4274
www.Xlibris.com
Orders@Xlibris.com
27325

This book is dedicated to my little granddaughter, Maya, in the hope she will come to know her grandfather more and more as the years go by.

Contents

Precious piece of protoplasm
Helpless heap of growing stuff
Flaps about the air
In wild gesticulation.

Button bounded by a belly
Full of gas and gurgle
Every sight is pure delight
To eyes that gape and ogle.

Introduction

As the saying goes, "Just because you're older, it doesn't mean you can't be immature." Well, that's me. I've been fortunate to grow older without growing up, and for that I have only my patients to thank. You see, I'm a pediatrician.

I liken my work-a-day world to a giant kind of amusement park. There are the visitors to the park—the "little people"; the "fun house" itself, my office; and the "house of horrors," the hospital. Each day is like a trip on a roller coaster with all of the excitement, exhilaration, twists and turns, and ups and downs of a ride that leaves one thrilled yet sometimes all too glad the experience is over. And there is the pageant of "little people," who parade through the amusement park in a never-ending stream, determined to endure or resist, to suffer, or enjoy, excited and frightened at the same time. Over the years my amusement park has seen its hodgepodge of little faces and little voices, and has given me enough anecdotes and vignettes, triumphs and tragedies to spin quite a tale. It's presented a kaleidoscope I wouldn't change for the world.

The work has proven stimulating and sometimes stressful, often humorous and sometimes sad, but never dull, and the characters I've met were always unique and incomplete, giving me the opportunity to see and help them unfold in the most surprising and delightful ways.

One of my greatest pleasures has been to chronicle the development of these little people through art. After all, amusement parks are not without their sidewalk artists. Our office too had its own, and it was me. On occasion, a quiet hiatus in an otherwise frenetic schedule gave me an opportunity to capture a patient's likeness on paper. The rendering was, for the most part, of creatures in perpetual motion. The resulting images were, therefore, accurate or distorted as time permitted or the mood suggested, and they were often repeated, in some cases over a number of years. In this way I had become the amusement park's official portrait artist, caricaturist, and historian. Some artists have their work exhibited in museums and galleries. My work, which I gave to the parents, has been hung on refrigerators. In this way I have become known as "the refrigerator artist."

What follows is an attempt to illustrate, in word and picture, a small but representative part of my world over the past thirty-five years. I have chosen stories that I thought would illustrate the wide variety of experiences I've encountered in my "park." The stories are true—although, in most cases, the names have been changed.

It's my hope that those who visit "the park" will share in a journey of humor and pathos and gain some insight into the world of that most feared and beloved of all creatures—the pediatrician.

That's My Belly Button

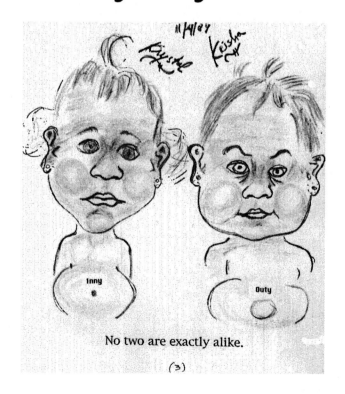

No two are exactly alike.

(3)

If there's one thing that separates pediatrics from other fields of medicine, it's this—everything the pediatrician looks at is examined against a backdrop of change. The sine qua non of children is growth and development, and when this does not occur there's usually a problem.

One item that changes little, however, even in pediatrics, is the belly button. Once the umbilical cord has separated and the belly button has dried, it remains immutable, unmovable, and unnoticed. It is, perhaps, the most taken-for-granted part of our anatomy.

But like so many things we take for granted, the belly button offers us opportunities. If we look closely, we will find the belly button to be a window to a child's personality. That's why I ask the following questions. Strange as it may seem, the following conversations really happened.

What's that? *(Pointing to belly button.)*
(As if he didn't hear) What?
(Pointing again) That.
(Quizzically) This?
Yes, that. What is it?
You're kidding. Right?
(Seriously) No, I'm not kidding. Really. What is it?
(Incredulously) C'mon. **You** know.
No. No, I don't know. What is it?
(Triumphantly) That's my belly button. *(He guffaws.)*

What's that? *(Pointing to belly button.)*
That's my neighbor. *(Navel??)*

Is that your belly button? *(Pointing to silver shirt button overlying belly.)*
No, it's not.
(With assurance) It must be your belly button. Look, it's silver. It's got writing on it.
(Makes a face.) You're silly.
(Emphatically) It **must** be your belly button. Look, it's on your belly. It's a button. Therefore, that's your belly button.
(As if to say—You don't know what you're talking about) **This is my belly button.** Look, there's a tattoo on it!

Who gave it to you?
(Cynically) It was there all the time.
(Skeptically) No, it wasn't. You can tell me. Where'd you get it? At Kmart?
(There is the beginning of a sly smile) No.
Then where?
I got it from **no**where. *(Giggles)*
I bet it was a birthday present. *(Pauses)* Was it?
Nah, it wasn't a birthday present. *(Getting second thoughts)* Was it, Mommy?

Was it a birthday present?
(Silence)
Was it? Was it?
(Says nothing.)
Can I have it?
(Turns head away.)
Can I? Pretty please with sugar on it.
(Almost in tears) It can't come off.

Where'd you get it?
(Flippantly) At the gas station. There's gum on it.

Where'd you get it?
(Puts on a serious face) From God.

Where'd you get it?
(Matter-of-factly) I think somebody shot me.

That your belly button?
Yep.
What's it for?
Nuffen.
Nuffen?
Yep, nuffen.

What do you do with it?
(Thinks for a moment) Take it off.
And then what?
(Without hesitation) Put it on again.

What do you do with it?
I take a bath with it.

What's it for anyhow?
I catch lint with it.

Your brother got one? *(Points to his belly button.)*
Yep.
Your sister?
Yep.

Your mommy?
Yep.
Your daddy?
Everybody gots one.
So who's got the nicest one in the family?
The dog.

Your sister got one?
Yes.
Your daddy?
Uh hmmm.
Who's got the nicest?
Daddy.
Why's that?
"'Cause you can stick your finger in it.

Can I have it?
(Resolutely) No!
(Pleadingly) Can I? Please?
Everybody gots one.
I never got one. Really.
Oh yeah? Let's see! *(Tries to lift up my shirt.)*
Can I have it?
(Resolutely.) No.
Can I? Please?
No. *(This time, louder.)*
That's not fair. If I had one and you asked me for it, I'd give it
    to you.
No. *(A brick wall this time.)*
Why not?
(Possessively, and with finality) 'Cause it's mine! *(And that's
    that!)*

Can I have it?

No.

Well then, can I borrow it? I'll give it back next time you come.

(Telling me why) It won't come off.

Yes, it will. I've got a belly button machine. I can take it off, and it won't even hurt *(Pleadingly)* Please?

OK.

Can I have it?

Sure, here. *(Pretends he removes his belly button and hands it over.)*

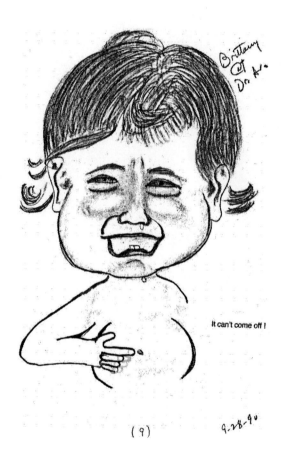

It can't come off !

(9)   9-28-90

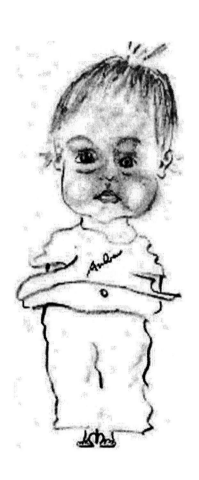

Changes

In thirty-five years of medical practice I've seen a lot of changes—some for the better, some for the worse. As our office grew in patient numbers, space, and size of staff, so did the demands placed on the doctor. For me it was a change from doctor working as doctor to doctor as doctor and CEO, efficiency expert, insurance and retirement fund planner, personnel manager, contract negotiator, and business person. Following are but a few of the many areas where I have observed significant changes.

House Calls

Oh, for the earlier days! I liked the days when a doctor was just a doctor. I liked making house calls. Though they were not a major part of our practice when I began, their numbers were significant, and their impact was immense. I always felt I learned more about a family in one house call than I did in ten office visits. Sharing coffee and conversation with parents in the middle of the night, sharing concern about their sick child created a bond of unusual strength and gave us an understanding and insight into the dynamics of the families we would never have had if we had never been to the home.

House calls went a long way toward establishing a feeling of trust between the parents and the doctor. I remember Michael, a father who called me one night at 2 a.m. shortly after I joined the practice. His daughter had spiked a high temperature, and he insisted I come over right away. As we discussed over the phone whether there was a true need for a house call, Michael suddenly became angry and stated loudly, "Doctor, I want you here now!" The child's symptoms suggested her illness did not require an emergency visit, but the parents' concern did, so I decided to go. When I got to the home, the father was soft-spoken. The mother, having heard her husband's conversation, appeared embarrassed and somewhat sheepish. By the time I left the house, both parents were reassured. They were relaxed and appeared truly grateful. My having made the trip told them I was concerned and available, and that I could be trusted to take care of their daughter, and, I might add, my judgment was never called into question by that family again.

When I was young, I had pneumonia, and our doctor made a house call. The doctor said, "I'm afraid we'll have to put him in the hospital."

"You can't do that, Doctor," said my grandmother. "He's too sick."

"We don't put well kids in the hospital," replied the doctor.

For some parents, there is still a fear of taking a sick child outside. Other parents feel doctors have stopped doing house calls to make life more convenient for themselves. It **is** true house calls are more time consuming and less convenient for the doctor. But we now know there is so much more we can do for a child in the office—using the laboratory for diagnosis or machines or injectables for treatment.

One can reasonably argue if a child is truly sick in the middle of the night, he should not be seen in his house or in the doctor's office for that matter but in the hospital where X rays, laboratory and emergency treatments are at hand.

Hospitals and House Staff

In my training and in the early years of pediatric practice, the private practitioner did everything. I remember performing bone marrow aspirations and exchange transfusions that are now performed mainly by hematologists and neonatologists. When a two-pound baby was born in the middle of the night, I was at the hospital, checking the baby at birth, arranging oxygen and an incubator, drawing bloods, and starting intravenous therapy. In those days we managed patients with leukemia, meningitis, and diabetes.

But nothing stays the same and certainly medicine has changed more rapidly and radically than many other fields. Knowledge has multiplied exponentially, and procedures have been developed for specialists who, by training and experience, can perform them exceptionally well. For the most part these changes represent "progress"; but for all that's been gained in subspecialty medicine, there's been something lost as well. Lost are some of those special relationships the patient once had with his/her doctor, and some of the continuity of care associated with one-doctor medicine. Today we no longer take care of the whole patient. We say that medicine has become increasingly compartmentalized.

Now a patient who is taken to an emergency room is likely to be seen by someone he doesn't know and who doesn't know him. If that patient is referred to a subspecialist, that doctor ideally has special knowledge and expertise pertaining to the patient's medical problem but may belong to a hospital that denies privileges to the patient's own personal physician.

Patients requiring close medical supervision in the hospital, who were once taken care of by their personal physicians, are now attended to by interns or residents in training. These doctors take medical histories, perform examinations, and often decide on tests to be performed and medicines to be given, though usually after consultation with the private physician by telephone. The interns and residents, who work and train in the hospitals, are there courtesy of the new alliances between medical school teaching programs and community hospitals. They are Johnnies-on-the-spot when it comes to emergencies in the hospital. And the private physician, who used to get up and run to the ward for every problem, now has only to discuss a patient's problem over the phone with an intern or resident before visiting his patient in the hospital the following morning.

New Technologies

It's a brave new world, and we might as well face it. The modern medical office doesn't have cyborgs performing doctor or secretarial functions; but it does have strange-looking robots lacking arms and legs but with great big brains to collate and store data. We call these mechanical miracles computers, and it's their job to file away information—not in drawers or cabinets but in cyberspace. They only ask that we feed them, and they're happy to work. The potential of the computer is astounding, and its usefulness will only continue to grow in medicine. I predict that in the United States, in but a few years, all physicians will graduate medical school speaking "computer"—and then will only have to learn to speak English as a second language when they enter the working world.

Technology has invaded the medical laboratory too—allowing us to obtain more information better, quicker, and faster in our own offices. We can learn if a patient has a strept throat infection—it used to take two-three days to do this—in a few minutes with reasonable accuracy now. New instrumentation allows us to treat asthmatics with inhalation therapy, a more effective treatment that often eliminates the need for shots or hospitalization.

The technology of telecommunications has advanced medical care as well. Pagers, and later, cellular phones, have greatly enhanced the doctor's accessibility, while at the same time, freeing him to attend to his own personal needs. Before these instruments were available, I stayed pretty much at home, tied to a telephone. It was not unusual on an on-call night, when I received a call while travelling, to have to pull off the highway to stop at a phone booth in freezing weather—and heaven help me if I didn't have any change. With the advent of the cellular phone, I was no longer required to stay home on nights I was on call. Nor to have change in my pocket when I was out of the house. On rare occasions when I found myself in a theater when on call I used a silent pager. A phone call alerted me through a vibration without disturbing those around me. I kept the pager close to my heart so that if I was disturbed by a phone call at least I got a thrill.

Health Care Delivery Systems

There's been a big change in the structure of health care delivery in the United States—away from private insurance companies and toward HMOs. Health Maintenance Organizations (HMOs) were originally established on the premise that if premiums were fixed, incomes would result from maintaining the lowest cost. It would then be in the best interest of the insurance company and its physicians to keep the policyholders well and out of the hospitals where the costs are highest. In the ideal, an HMO would profit through wellness maintenance. The concept was a good one; however, the devil was in the details. To increase profits, some HMOs looked to insure only the healthiest populations and discouraged laboratory tests, doctor referrals, and costly hospitalizations. Our office signed on early with a number of HMOs, not knowing how the new system would be received and not wanting to lose any patients who would be required by their employers to join an HMO. The move to the new method of delivery was not always a smooth one and resulted in a loss of patient continuity, since some patents opted to go to HMOs paid for by their employers, which we were not servicing. I remember we were at one time servicing more than thirty different plans. Our connection with HMOs was not always without incident. It took some adjusting. I remember being challenged on my judgment to refer a patient to a dermatologist by an HMO administrator.

"Dr. Aronson," the administrator said. "You referred Tommy Barkley to Dr. Zinn, the dermatologist."

"Yes," I replied.

"Don't you think you could take care of it yourself?"

"If I did I wouldn't be referring Tommy. It's an unusual rash, and I think it may need a biopsy."

"It's not our policy to refer any rash to a dermatologist. Most rashes can be taken care of in the regular physician's office."

"Pardon me, Doctor," I stated. "Are you a dermatologist? Are you currently practicing pediatrics?"

"I'm the administrator of the plan, and if I say I want to see her I want to see her. You just have her call my office for an appointment."

I had been in practice for thirty years at the time. The administrator would not agree to a referral until he saw the patient himself. After seeing the patient, he agreed the referral was justified. This left the patient angry at the inconvenience and confused over the need.

The above experience shows the difficulty of dealing with an HMO bureaucracy, which can be inflexible and arbitrary and carries with it its own set of laws, requirements, restrictions, and payments. We made many attempts to evaluate the pros and cons of servicing each, dropped a couple and considered keeping others. The factors to be considered were so varied and complex, in the end we ended up with our gut feelings when it came to deciding to keep or terminate our relationship with an HMO.

Economics

As the saying goes, "Some years ago my grandfather framed the first dollar he earned in a ten-cent frame. Today, that ten-cent frame costs one dollar, and the dollar is worth only ten cents." Contrary to Plato, there are no absolutes in this world. But there may be one—over the years prices will go up.

In the early days of practice our expense ratio was 33 percent, meaning of every dollar received, thirty-three cents was spent to run the office. Today the expense ratio is approaching 55 percent despite heroic efforts to keep it down. The largest increases in costs were, for us, in the area of drugs, salaries, and hospital and malpractice insurance, and salaries.

When I attended medical school, the tuition (a state school) was $200 to $300 per quarter. Though physically difficult, it was possible to work part time and to pay for medical school without going into debt. Medical books, which were every bit as large and heavy then as they are now, were affordable and the only risk of having one was an hernia. Today, to own the required medical books one only risks bankruptcy. When I started my internship, my wife was pregnant and unemployed and my salary was $3200 per year, but we had accrued no debts and could scrape by on that salary. Today, medical students who come through our office in training tell us they are over $100,000 in debt.

A medical practice is first and foremost a service. But it is also a business. As in any business, the focus is on the bottom line, and a medical practice increases its charges to keep up with expenses. In an ordinary business the cost of a product is determined by the marketplace, but in the case of pediatrics other considerations are required. Sick children are entitled to care even when their parents have trouble paying the bill, and paying the bills is much more difficult for new families who are generally at the lower end of their earning curves. Despite the fact that fees have increased steadily over the years, the pediatrician's net income in our office remained stable over the past ten years.

The Litigious Society

Thirty-five years ago, when I started practicing pediatrics, our office carried $200,000 malpractice insurance for each doctor. Malpractice suits were rare in those days and $200,000 awards were considered high if not exorbitant or unlikely.

Today, if a doctor practices long enough, he'll get sued, and for far larger amounts, no matter how bright, competent, or conscientious he is. And the number of malpractice lawsuits far exceeds the number of bona fide cases of negligence.

Malpractice lawsuits have shown a steady rise in the past ten years and costs exceed $10,000,000,000 in claims with an estimated additional $15,000,000,000 in tests or procedures, which, in fact, may be unnecessary but are nevertheless ordered by physicians to protect themselves from lawsuits. The problem has increased for the following reasons (among others):

1. With the advent of group practices and the increased use of emergency rooms, it's now more likely patients see, from time to time, a doctor with whom they are unfamiliar. Hence, there has been no relationship established, increasing the likelihood of a lack of trust.

2. The rapid development of new technologies may have contributed to unrealistic expectations of what medicine and doctors can do for people,

3. Medical costs have skyrocketed, causing a desperation in some families for funds, especially those confronted with catastrophic illness, and media reports of astronomical awards make the idea of lawsuit enticing.

To the doctor who has sacrificed years of early earnings in hard study and sacrifice, and who has made his every decision to the best of his ability, and with the intent of helping his patients, a suit against him falls very hard. Where literally thousands of decisions are required in the face of an ever-present danger that one of them could lead to a lawsuit, the day-to-day practice of medicine becomes, for many, unenjoyable if not intolerable.

Twenty-five years ago, two doctors in our practice were sued for malpractice (along with two surgeons and a hospital.) One of my partners who was sued had nothing to do with the patient's care other than to sign the discharge order in the patient's chart when it was time to leave the hospital. At that time, the limits on our malpractice insurance were $200,000 per doctor. The patients—who were suing for $5,000,000— were willing to settle with us for the limits of our policies. Our insurance company, who felt we had done no wrong, also felt that with the uncertainty of jury verdicts and the amount of exposure, we should settle. So the case was settled for each of the two doctors. Subsequently, the malpractice rates were increased for all five doctors in our practice, and those new rates formed a base for every succeeding rate increase over the next twenty-five years (and into the future). Our increased rates were passed on to the patients in increased fees, illustrating how the cost of malpractice compounds and multiplies.

Here is an extreme example of the kind of antagonistic relationship, which I see being encouraged by the litigious society and the cynical media. Sometime ago I saw an eleven-year-old boy who was a newcomer to our practice. In the course of the physical exam I did to him what I've done to many of the children I'd examined over my thirty-five years of practice. I held his arm so his hand drooped, told him not to move his finger, pointing to the precise finger, then tapped his forearm and watched the finger jump. The reflex usually amuses the child and relaxes him for the rest of the examination. I then brushed the top of his head and said, "I told you not to move that finger. Now don't move that finger," I said once again, pointing to the exact finger. And I repeated the procedure, watching the finger jump once more, and then brushing the child across his head when it moved. The mother responded with a stern, "Don't hit my kid!" I looked at her and said, in surprise, "I'm sorry. I didn't think it would bother you. I didn't hurt him. I was playing with him like I do so many kids, but if you don't like it I won't do it." Their visit had run into a good part of the lunch hour so after it was over, I left the office to run an errand. When I returned, two policemen were waiting for me. I was being charged with assault and battery. After discussing the episode with the police, the patient, and his parents, the parents were dissuaded from pressing charges. I told the story to one of my partners and she stated, "That's why I don't play with the kids anymore."

One of my "mothers" in the practice is a school principal. She tells me that hardly a week goes by that the police aren't called into the schoolyard over a fight between two students—often seven or eight years old.

There are pediatric offices where no child is examined in an undressed state without someone in the room for fear of being sued for molestation.

It **has** become a litigious society and that's truly sad.[1]

---

[1] This is not to say malpractice isn't an ever-present threat, and some cases of severe damages involve gross negligence and demand settlements in very high figures.

Expertitis

Like others, my amusement park had a "House of Mirrors." Who hasn't had the experience of looking into a mirror to find the image magnified? The experience is not uncommon to doctors who are looked up to as experts, even when they're not. The following story happened to me and clearly illustrates how people, searching for an authority, appeal to a doctor for expert opinions, only to find those opinions, like reflections in a mirror, may become distorted and somehow "larger than life." The following story, written by me in 1974, was published in the *Chicago Journalism Review* and later distributed nationwide in the *Epidemiology Information Newsletter* of the Communicable Disease Center in Atlanta.

If the press needs "new blood" for the treatment of its ills, then here I am. As a pediatrician, I've had considerable experience with communication and behavior disorders.

Not long ago I received a phone call from my sister-in-law, Anne Keagan, who writes for the Chicago Tribune. *"Neil," she said, "What do you know about Reye's Syndrome?" I told her that I didn't know much, but that it was an illness with severe liver and brain involvement, affecting children and often fatal. I also mentioned that it was extremely rare and only recently described in the medical literature, and that it would therefore be hard to find much written about it in the medical textbooks. Anne then mentioned a* Tribune *reporter was having trouble getting information. I offered to check my files at home and within a matter of minutes had located the information and was back on the phone with the reporter discussing various aspects of this medical phenomenon that had apparently invaded our Chicago community.*

I emphasized that the cause was unknown though felt to be related, perhaps, in some way to viral infections; extremely rare (only 120 cases had been in the world literature as of 1970); and sometimes fatal.

If I knew then what I know now, I wouldn't have mentioned (as an aside) that influenza B virus had been isolated from the liver of one patient who died with Reye's Syndrome—and that one could speculate about the high incidence of Reye's in the area in light of the widespread influenza B epidemic that was sweeping the community.

That evening I received a phone call from a reporter who stated, "Dr. Aronson, this is so-and-so from the Daily News. There's an article quoting you on the first page of tomorrow's Tribune regarding Reye's Syndrome. Do you mind if I ask you a few questions?" I was surprised to hear I'd become an authority on this rare disease and when I gathered my wits about me (or perhaps I should say before I gathered my wits about me), I replied, "Why no, go right ahead."

Once again, I found myself explaining the disease and its manifestations. Before our conversation ended, I asked the reporter if he would read the Tribune's article. I was stupefied. "Good grief," I said to myself (and later to the reporter) "that article could scare the bejeesas out of every mother [literal meaning intended] in the community." In the middle of an epidemic I was afraid the article would be widely misread, and so I attempted to secure a promise from the Daily News *reporter that certain information would be emphasized in the hopes of offsetting a near likely panic.*

I then called Anne to tell her I had just heard from the Daily News. *"That's really crazy," said Anne. "I swear, reporters are like lemmings. They saw your name in the paper and just naturally rushed to you as if you were the sea." I then expressed my own doubts over the* Tribune *article, that I felt it could be misread and frightening, and I learned that an editor had already read the article and had called the paper to express fear for his own sick child. The article was toned down and appeared in later editions of the* Tribune *the following day in what I felt was a more acceptable form.*

That following morning I received a phone call from WLS radio asking me if I would be willing to answer a few questions for the radio audience about Reye's Syndrome. I then explained I never did research in the disease, never had a case in my own practice, and, in fact, would probably never have been quoted if I didn't happen to have a sister-in-law who was a reporter for the Tribune.

When we went on the air, I was introduced as a prominent physician [thank you] from the University of Chicago [which I'm not] who had done years of research in Reye's Syndrome. (As luck would have it, the one thing the broadcaster got right in the interview was my name.)

I was asked to describe the illness. And then, with incredible directness and in a manner hardly calculated to "soothe" the community twitch, the broadcaster asked, "Doctor, can you tell our listeners what they can do for their children who now have the flu to prevent this fatal illness?"

Later that day I received calls from all over the country—Long Beach, California; Cleveland, Ohio; Mississippi; Washington DC; and Ottawa, Canada. People whose children died from or survived Reye's Syndrome called to give me information, hoping that in some way it might save lives. I was asked to appear on a television show and to speak to a community gathering.

I felt myself battered about like a row boat in the rough and swirling seas of instant and modern communication. My ego, however, received a great lift when I was called by a reporter from NBC news. Seemingly contradictory statements had apparently been made—one by Dr. Henry Nadler, professor and head of pediatrics for Northwestern Medical School and chief of service at Children's Memorial Hospital; the other by Dr. Peter Hutenlocher, an expert from Yale University, a reputed authority on Reye's, and one who had come to Chicago to help with the treatment of this disease.

The reporter asked me, "Dr. Aronson, perhaps you can straighten us out on this point." He then proceeded to tell me that Dr. Nadler said this and Dr. Huttenlocher said that. "Dr. Aronson," he said, "which one is right?"

At this point, I received what I would call a "media gestalt." Not only had the media created its own expert, it actually believed him.

Erica

Erica was two-and-a-half years old and her baby sister, Sarah, was six months. Like most two-year-olds, Erica was an explorer. That's why she disappeared in our office one day while I was examining her sister. When we realized she was gone, Inez—her mother—and I set off to find her, and it wasn't long before she turned up. She was, as they say, a little dickens.

When the examinations were completed and it was time to go, Inez couldn't find her wallet. "I've got everything in my wallet," Inez said, "my identification and credit cards, my driver's license, a set of my house keys—even a list of things to do today and for the remainder of this week. I know I had it when I left the house this morning."

We searched high and low for the wallet, checking the front desk where Inez registered her children, and the examining room—especially around the area where Inez had set her purse. Erica, realizing we were looking for something, helped us— crawling on her hands and knees, looking under the table, opening drawers and such. To her it was a delightful game we were playing.

But Inez wasn't delighted. She was perplexed and quite visibly upset. When she got home, she would have to arrange for changing all her locks and then set out to get copies of her identification and credit cards.

Inez returned with Erica for another exam in six months. In the interim I had called her on a few occasions (she's my cousin) to learn if she had found the wallet. Many times I reassured her it could not possibly be in our office since the end of each day found the office looking as if it had just barely survived "the blitz," and every night it was completely cleaned by our crews, who were very thorough and surely would have found it.

After Erica's examination and while Inez and I were discussing family news, Erica left the room. A short time later she returned—this time with her mother's wallet.

We never learned where Erica put the wallet—and unfortunately, after that time, I never fully trusted the job that was done by our cleaning service.

Caught in the Middle

Sometimes one just "hits it off" with a family. That's the way it was with Bob and Jean Edwards and their children, Ronald and Emily. For me, Bob and Jean were just easy to be with, and a visit with them usually meant a relaxed and pleasant conversation. Ronald was an interesting contradiction in terms— with a mop of straight hairs in wild disarray, while at the same time, impeccably neat; and Emily was always smiling and lively to the point of exuberance. One day when Bob and Jean entered my office with a rather serious look on their faces (not their usual cheerful selves), I knew there was something pressing on their minds. I didn't have to wait too long to find out.

After I finished routine examinations of Ronald and Emily, Bob and Jean asked me to accompany them into our library. (There's something about a library. We had complete privacy in my office, but one whispers in a library, augmenting an air of confidentiality to the visit.)

No sooner were we in the library, Bob handed me a pamphlet. He said, "Take a look at this." A cursory look at the pamphlet indicated the material had something to do with Jehovah's Witnesses. I looked at the pamphlet for some time.

"What do you think of it?" Jean asked. She had an expectant look on her face.

"I'm not sure I understand your question," I replied, not knowing whether they were looking for an opinion—or, indeed, were trying to convert me.

"Go ahead, read a little more," said Bob. The material focused, in the main, on what appeared to be dietary laws forbidding the ingestion of blood, as set down in the Old Testament. In a broader sense, the material prohibited the taking into the body, in any way, any blood or blood products, e.g., blood transfusions. "I don't believe we ever told you we are Jehovah's Witnesses."

"No, you didn't," I replied, still not quite sure where the conversation was heading.

"What would you do if our kids needed a transfusion?" Bob then asked. (The cat was out of the bag.)

I paused, for a moment, to consider. "I'd give them one," I answered.

"But you can see in the papers we gave you, our religion forbids it. It's against our religious beliefs."

"I respect your beliefs," I said. "But you see, I swore an oath to uphold life, which means I would have to insist on a transfusion."

"But we'd never allow that," said Jean. "We can't do anything that goes against our religion." Jean appeared quite upset.

"Well, I can understand that. But your children are too young to have decided that **they** are Jehovah's witnesses. Society takes another view, and in it, the law doesn't recognize your right, even as parents, to make life-and-death decisions on their behalf."

"So then, in the event one of our kids needs a transfusion, what happens?"

"To be frank with you, what happens is you tell me you won't allow a transfusion for Ron or Emily—that you won't allow this for religious reasons. Then I, having sworn an oath to uphold life, and feeling your decision threatens the life of your child, given the law, am obligated to refer the problem to a social worker, who obtains a court order appointing your children wards of the state. The state orders a transfusion, effectively taking the decision out of your hands."

"But they're our kids. And this is our religion."

"The state recognizes that. And I do too. But this is the law. It's what the law would force me to do." Their expressions darkened. They were hurt, and my heart went out to them. "Look," I said, "I know this is very hard on you. I respect your religious beliefs. And you know how much I love the kids. But I have to follow the law—and I really do think it's the right thing to do."

"In that case, we can't bring our children here anymore. We'll just have to find a doctor who'll let us practice our religion," they said. Bob and Jean exchanged looks as if to confirm they were in total agreement, and then simply walked out with their children.

I never saw them again. I missed Ronald's wild mop of hair and Emily's lively spirit and happy smile. I wonder what happened to them. I hope they never needed a blood transfusion. I wonder if they found a doctor who would truly respect their wishes, or if they were seeing a doctor who merely said he would, knowing full well the likelihood of their ever needing a transfusion was extremely low. Would that same doctor, in the event a transfusion was needed, change his position?

My experience with the Edwards family, which was my first experience of this sort, showed me an example of the complexity of medical practice when it intersects with the law. It also showed how the law protects the doctor, as well as the child, in a case where the appropriate course of action for a doctor is clearly proscribed, and when the right to religious freedom conflicts with the Hippocratic Oath.

The experience raised an interesting question. Under what circumstances, if any, is a child able to act on his own behalf, according to that child's religious belief?

James

James was so difficult he gave "contrary" a good name. He was willful and incorrigible, oftentimes appearing as if he were on a mission to oppose.

When I was new to pediatric practice, I always thought if a patient was referred to me it meant that someone valued or respected me or my services, but after spending a few minutes with James I couldn't help but wonder what heinous crime I had committed to have been recommended to him. Being in a room with James was punishment with a capital *P*.

James' mother brought him into the office the first time. She was smallish, thin and frazzled, and appeared tense, as if she was on guard—about to be attacked. Her eyes darted about her, and she spoke in short clipped sentences.

"We don't know what to do about our son," she said. She then turned her attention to her son and said, "James, stay away from that phone. James, this time I mean it." I looked at James, and when I turned my attention back to his mother, she continued, "He's only eight years old and already we've had him in five different schools. They don't keep him for long. He's bright, they tell me, but he just—James, stay away from that telephone. I said put that phone down. See what I mean, Doctor? He just doesn't listen." James was thin and wiry, and his lips showed the slightest hint of a smile. He turned his attention to a stethoscope on my desk. "James," said his mother, "those are the doctor's instruments. Don't touch." James continued playing with the stethoscope, looking at his mother with that hint of a smile, until she walked over to him and yanked the instrument from his hands. "Sorry, Doctor," she said, then turning her attention to her son, "James, sit over there" (pointing to chairs by the window).

"As you can see, Doctor, he hears, but he doesn't listen." By this time James was standing on a chair leaning against the window. Our office was on the fifth floor. "James, sit down. It's dangerous. You'll fall out." James answered her request by pounding on the window. His mother then pulled him out of the chair and dragged him to a corner of the room, saying, "Now you stand here or I'm going to get your father." If anything, James's smile became more pronounced. "I'm sorry, Doctor, his father thought it best if he waited outside—in your waiting room. Maybe I'd better get him."

After his mother left, James took a tentative step out of the corner into the room, watching me closely to see how I might respond. I did nothing and remained silent.

At that moment, the parents returned. I was introduced to James's father, who was about six feet five inches tall and thick, and if that wasn't intimidating enough, wore a scowl, an expression that appeared to be etched in his face. James looked at his father, then ran to my desk, and grabbed a pen. He then quickly moved to our examination table and began scribbling on it. Fortunately, our tables are covered with white paper so no permanent harm was done.

James's father clearly was on a short fuse. He walked over to James. He lifted him up as if he was no more than a small stick (compared to his father he was no more than a small stick), and he forcefully set him down in a chair saying, "Behave yourself, and I mean it!"

James hit his father.

The rest of the medical history, and the physical exam, went in bits and snatches. I learned that James, who had been expelled from five schools for "aberrant behavior" had seen numerous psychologists and psychiatrists, and had been on many medications—all to no avail. The physical exam, not performed without interruptions, or difficulty, was as I expected, normal.

At the end of the visit, I told James's parents I could see the problem they were having and that I wanted to help. James was depriving himself of an education and deserved a life where people would like him and respond positively to him. But his problems were more severe than I had seen, and I wasn't quite sure what to do. I suggested they call me in a week after I had a chance to do a little more reading and make some calls.

I didn't hear from James's parents in one week. But I did see them four months later when they came to my office with James. As I recall, we talked for about fifteen minutes. James was doing well in school for the first time. There had been a sea change in his behavior, and it was evident in his visit this time. He was quiet, cooperative, and respectful.

It turned out James had been sent to a military academy. I was told the first day he was there he smeared feces on the wall of the cafeteria.[2] I'm not certain how the school responded to that, or to any other misdeeds James most probably committed, but the positive effects of those few months in the school were obvious.

I'm not advocating military schools, I have no knowledge or experience in this area, I'm certain there are military schools with differing approaches and of different quality, and I don't know what the long-term effects of James's experience in military school will be. The solution, in most cases, is not so quick or easy.

I suppose if I learned one thing from my experience with James it was this, the stress and pain of a parent who lives with a child who exhibits severe deviant behavior is enormous.

My heart goes out to those parents whose every day is a heroic struggle. These people deserve our respect and support.

---

[2]   Such behavior is generally indicative of a deep-seated psychiatric disturbance and not one likely to improve so dramatically over so short a period of time.

Gary–A Boy with Hemophilia

Gary was a patient of mine when I was in training as an intern. He was twelve years old, quite good looking, and very bright. He lived with his mother Mary who was single. Gary had hemophilia.

Gary's hemophilia, the "classical" variety, meant he was lacking a specific chemical in his bloodstream necessary for clotting, subjecting him to the danger of serious, perhaps fatal bleeding following minor injury. Classical hemophilia is hereditary, transmitted in a sex-linked fashion, which means females carry the illness; males get it. This added a psychological dimension to Gary's illness in that his mother could feel responsible for his having it. Episodes of bleeding are recurrent and some occur spontaneously.

Bleeding is often noted in the first days of life with excessive bleeding following circumcision, and commonly, later, with the onset of walking (and falling.) On occasion, excessive bleeding occurs during eruption or loss of deciduous teeth. In the hemophiliac, bleeding may occur anywhere: from the mucus membranes into muscles, organs, brain, or body cavities. Joint cavities are commonly involved, usually ankles, knees and elbows. Bleeding occurs cyclically, and recurrent hemorrhages eventually cause damage to the synovial membranes of joints, with destruction to the articular surfaces and erosion of bone. Treatment consists of local measures and rapid blood or blood factor replacement.

Gary was admitted to the hospital on numerous occasions when I was in training there—usually for bleeding into his knees. He tried hard to be brave, and though he was often in pain and never too fond of needles, he rarely complained. In the course of caring for him on his frequent admissions, I often learned of his disappointments—the party or celebration he was missing, the events he couldn't attend, not to mention the everyday activities young boys engage in which were always off-limits to him.

Gary made up for his disappointments by writing. He was gifted with intelligence, language, and imagination, and his stories often involved a hero who had become weakened in some way, often near death, but who was saved "in the nick of time" through the injection of a miraculous substance into his blood. These stories were clearly a form of wish fulfillment, and their transparency made them all the more meaningful.

It must have been some ten years after I finished my training. My wife and I had moved to Chicago. I got a phone call from Gary. He was in Chicago, remembered I lived there, looked me up, and wanted to visit me. Of course I was thrilled to hear from him. He wasn't far from our house when he called, and we decided he should come right over. After hanging up the phone, I had some misgivings. At the time, I lived in an apartment building and on a high second-floor walk-up. It occurred to me, not having seen him in ten years, he might not be able to manage the stairs. Would he come with friends to carry him up? I started thinking I should have met him somewhere else, but I had no way to contact him, and he was already on his way.

Our doorbell rang. Gary walked up the stairs on his own. At that time, not having had any hemophiliac patients in our practice, I was unaware of the newer, more purified and potent clotting factors and blood products that were available to him, and the arrangements that were made for some patients who were knowledgeable and capable to initiate treatment at home—advances that had an astounding effect on limiting the destructive effect of his illness.

Gary, who was a good-looking boy, had become a handsome young man. I learned he was going to medical school. We enjoyed a short conversation in which he relived his hospitalizations, reminding me of things I might have said or did, which I had long since forgotten, and I reminded him of the many stories he had written and shared with me on the ward.

Despite the differences in our age I felt it was a meeting of old friends. I was thrilled to see Gary so well and excited about his future. I hoped that, in some way, the quality of our relationship had something top do with his career choice.

This was the first time (and only time) one of my Cleveland patients visited me. As I think about it, perhaps, in Gary's mind I was the one who injected that miraculous medicine into his blood. I realize that what I did for him many others would have done also. No more no less. But I was his doctor, and I was the one who did it and that accident of fate made it possible for us to form a unique bond based on shared concern and human contact.

I've lost touch with Gary. It's been a long time. I'm concerned about the course of his hemophilia. I wonder how he's doing. He must surely have graduated by now. I wonder what field of medicine he chose. Did he decide to become a pediatrician so he could take care of children? Did he decide to become a hematologist so he could apply his brilliance and interest in an area related, perhaps, to his own problem. I'm sure, whatever field he's chosen, he'll bring to it the benefit of his experience as a patient along with his compassion and understanding.

Good luck, Gary. The world is lucky to have you.

Mothers

In commenting about pediatrics as a career choice, most of my friends tell me they think they would love the work, but they have one large reservation. "I love the kids," they say, "but how do you deal with the mothers?" It's interesting they don't ask me how I deal with the fathers because I see plenty of fathers in my office too.

My father used to say facetiously, "Some women are all alike." Well, I've probably had 15,00 contacts with women (and men)over thirty-five years of pediatric practice, and I beg to differ. Although the many women who pass through my office do share some of the same basic concern, namely, the health of their children, they differ like night and day. Their personalities, their reactions occupy unique places on the spectrum of human behavior. I have categorized each of these mothers, who visit, flit through, and camp out in our office as one of the following:

the punctilious
the free spirit
the scholar
the unknowing
the oblivious
the hysterical
the historian
the skeptic

Of course, most mothers are some mixture of these types, but it's the combination of personality traits, along with the type that's predominant that determines the approach to mothering that will be most effective

The *Punctilious Mother* is never late. She could have been swept up in the vortex of a cyclone, she enters the office on time, dressed to the nines, without a hair out of place. She must have had an incredible toilet training period, she's so compulsive. The *Punctilious Mother* thrives on strict schedules and regimentation and when such a mother comes into the office with her newborn I tell her something like this, "Feed the baby at 3:00 p.m., 6:00 p.m., 9:00 p.m., midnight, 3:00 a.m., 6:00 a.m., 9:00 a.m., and noon," knowing full well she may be watching the minute hand of the clock waiting for the appropriate feeding moment. The important thing is that it's possible to reinforce the *Punctilious Mother's* natural tendencies to be exact to make her feel more comfortable with her mothering.

Not so the *Free Spirit Mother*. To give such a mother a strict feeding schedule is an exercise in the absurd and giving such a schedule to the *Free Spirit* is doomed to failure. The

Free Spirit is spontaneous and doesn't do well with authority figures. Free-spirited mothers treat their children like they do each of the hairs on their head, they let them go in any direction they want. Their kids are often treated with a form of "benign neglect," and, if these kids are resourceful, they grow up happy and independent. I recommend these mothers keep their "little puppies" on a very long leash but a leash nevertheless.

The *Scholar Mother* comes to the office loaded with information. This mother is a voracious reader of newspapers, magazine articles, books, and medical journal articles (when she can get her hands on them), and she's not averse to searching the Internet when the need arises. When speaking to the *Scholar Mother* who is not quite certain my suggestions are the way to go, I've found statements like these to be most effective:

"Haste and Barlow, in their monograph on teething from last month's *Archives of Pediatrics* had this to say, . . ."

"Actually there are a lot of approaches to this. Mine is based on my experience, which seems to make sense to me and has worked in a large number of cases."

"You appear to have trouble with my recommendations. Would you feel better if I referred you to Dr. So-and-So? He's considered something of an authority on this, and he might have an approach that you'll feel more comfortable with."

The *Scholar Mother* stands in stark contrast to the *Unknowing Mother* who is unsophisticated in her approach to child rearing but may turn out to be quite capable in her parenting. Where the *Scholar Mother* is intellectual, the

Unknowing Mother is more apt to be instinctual. The *Scholar Mother* flies by the instruction manual; the *Unknowing Mother* flies by the seat of her pants. The *Unknowing Mother* needs very special instructions. One such mother called me once to tell me the suppository I told her to give was too big and her child couldn't swallow it.

I've always found it a good idea to submit a detailed, written plan to the *Unknowing Mother* and to emphasize the need to maintain communication.

Where the *Unknowing Mother* doesn't know, the *Oblivious Mother* doesn't notice. These mothers are most difficult to get histories from, and they can't be relied upon to make good observations. I feel sorry for the *Oblivious Mother* because I can't help feeling she's missing out on the great joys of motherhood. Here is a place where the pediatrician can be most helpful by encouraging mindfulness, educating as to how development can be expected to occur (e.g., a grasp develops from batting at objects, more purposeful movements, bending of the hand and holding with all fingers folded, then, finally, to thumb and forefinger opposition) and enlisting the mother's efforts to aid in the child's development. That kind of teaching a pediatrician can give the *Oblivious Mother* is invaluable, but not one that we were taught in school.

The *Hysteric Mother* is one to whom the tiniest scratch is a cut, every cut is a laceration, and every laceration an amputation. For such mothers, every call to our office is a 911—a dire emergency. For children of *Hysteric Mothers*, whose every tummy ache is an intestinal obstruction, it's a difficult but critical thing to keep in mind that the mother can be right.

We quickly learn who these mothers are, but we can't write them off. Just because there's an epidemic of stomach flu in the community and every child we see in our office has abdominal pain, that doesn't mean **one** might not have appendicitis. In most cases the child of the *Hysteric Mother* has exactly what the others have. We treat him, and he gets better. The plus side of treating the child of a *Hysteric Mother* is that the *Hysteric Mother* feels her child is so sick, when we cure him she thinks we've saved his life. I'm certain there are no small number of children of *Hysteric Mothers* out there whose lives I saved many times.

On occasion, I read history books. Though often interesting, they're not my favorite books. I'm not a detail person, and history books are chock-full of details. So are the *Historian Mothers* who come through my office. On a busy day, a medical history from such a mother gives me fits. It usually goes something like this: "It started on Tuesday at 6:30 p.m., Doctor. He likes soup, and I was giving him soup. But he wouldn't take it. So I took his temperature and it was 102. At 10 p.m., it was 101, and I thought he was getting better. On Wednesday his fever was up and down—being highest at 8 p.m. when it was 103.5. At 7:00 a.m., Thursday he was cool, but at 3:00 p.m. it was 101. At 5:00, he was quite warm, and I took his temperature again. It was 104.5! This is Friday already. He was normal this morning, but here it is 3:45 and his fever is 101.7 and going higher. I don't know what to do." I tell her that fevers have their ups and downs and are usually highest in the late afternoon or early evening, and I'm tempted to tell her to throw the thermometer away. Her detailed history has taken up ten precious minutes of office time, and, although the specifics of her child's fevers seem important to her, I realize the details are not relevant to determine what her child has or needs for treatment.

I know I'm in for it when the *Historian Mother* comes into the office with her three children, all new patients, carrying reams of notes as if on a roll of toilet paper. The notes, covering the histories of her three children, in detail, are often recorded in a haphazard order and given as the three children jump, fight, and scream in the office.

The *Mother Skeptic* is another type I see in the office. I often think the group practice was especially made for these mothers as it gives them a chance to compare and play off what one doctor tells them against another. A typical conversation with a *Mother Skeptic* goes something like this:

DOCTOR: I'm going to give you a prescription for some medicine.
MOTHER: Does Mikey need a prescription?
DOCTOR: Yes. This will help him.
MOTHER: Are you sure?
DOCTOR: As sure as I can be. It should help Mikey feel better.
MOTHER: And what if it doesn't?
DOCTOR: But I think it will. At any rate, if it doesn't, which is unlikely, we can give him something else.
MOTHER: The last time you saw him he was sick, and you didn't give him anything—and he got better.
DOCTOR: The last time I saw him he didn't need medicine. I didn't give him any because it wouldn't have helped him.

The *Mother Skeptic*, like the *Scholar Mother*, often responds to printed literature. When she cannot be convinced that the recommended course of treatment is the correct one, a referral to a partner or perhaps a consultant is not inappropriate.

"How do you deal with the mothers?" ask my friends. Indeed, mothers enter the office anxious and sometimes angry. There are times when they appear to be uncaring, disbelieving, even neurotic to me, but it all goes into the mix. I've learned a lot from my mothers. They've perceived things in ways I never thought. They've helped me see things in different ways. I respect the forthright way they meet the challenges of parenthood. They're, for the most part, all good mothers, and I value the trust they've placed in me as their child's physician as well as the friendship I've made with them. "How do I deal with the mothers (and fathers)?" I've seen them all: the *punctilious,* the *free spirited,* the *scholars,* the *unknowing,* the *oblivious,* the *hysterics,* the *historians,* and the *skeptics*—and more.

It's the variety that makes pediatrics exciting, challenging, surprising, and never dull.

What's Your Secret, Kid?

One of the things I've enjoyed most about pediatrics has been the opportunity it's provided me to get to know families. And the better I've known them, the easier it's been to joke with them.

A case in point is Sally Templar, whose ten-year-old Johnny I had taken care of since birth. Sally and I had developed a close relationship over the years, and there were few things we couldn't talk about. As I was sitting at my desk, writing notes in Johnny's chart after an exam, she asked me, "What's wrong with Johnny, Doctor? He's always got an erection."

I immediately dropped my pen, pushed away from the desk, leaped across the room, closed my fingers around Johnny's neck, and said, "What's your secret, kid?"[3]

---

[3] Although such a finding may indicate an underlying medical problem, I assured Mrs. Templar her son Johnny was normal.

Nursemaid's Elbow

As a pediatrician, among some of the simplest and most satisfying things I did was to reduce a dislocated radial head, or, in layman's terms, fix a nursemaid's elbow.

A typical story usually went something like this. A mother was walking with her toddler, holding on to the hand. Perhaps, either because the toddler suddenly decided to stop, or to change direction, the arm is pulled. The child would often scream out, the arm become limp, and the child would then refuse to use it.

Think of the terror in the mind of a parent whose child suddenly appears to develop a paralyzed arm. The terror is compounded when the parent feels somewhat responsible.

On occasion, a child with nursemaid's elbow is x-rayed and the condition resolves itself. The correction occurs when the arm is manipulated in the course of taking the X ray. More often, however, a frantic call is made to the pediatrician who recommends the child be brought to the office. A brief medical history and examination makes the diagnosis, and manipulation of the arm cures the condition, often within minutes.

A pediatrician often works in unusual conditions. I cured one case in a parking lot. My experience has taught me the longer an elbow stays dislocated, the longer the discomfort after it's fixed. That's why I even repaired one over the telephone. Mandy Smith was a cute little three-year-old with golden locks that made it look like she'd just stepped out of "The Three Little Bears." I remember getting a call from her mother at 2:00 one morning.

"Mandy can't move her arm," said her mother. "Since when?" I asked, hoping I was coherent, having just awakened.

"Since a few minutes ago. She woke up screaming, and I couldn't comfort her. I tried to walk her around, and I was holding her hand. She tugged at my hand, then gave a little cry. Then her arm went limp and now she refuses to move it altogether. It looks like it hurts her."

"Can you bring her to the office? I'll meet you there."

"Oh, Doctor, I can't. My husband's out of town, and I've got four kids at home. I just can't wake them, dress them all, and take them to your office."

"Well it really has to be fixed—the sooner the better. Listen to what I have to say—very carefully. You may be able to fix this yourself, at home, if you do exactly what I say. It may hurt Mandy while you're doing it, but really just for a few seconds. Then she should be all better. Do you want to give it a try?"

"If you think I can do it, Doctor. Yes, I'll try."

"Good. Now, which arm is it?"

"It's her right arm, Doctor."

"OK then, let's start. I want you to tell me after you've done each thing I ask you to."

"She's sitting."

"Good. Now extend your left arm and take a firm hold of her right upper arm with your left arm and her right wrist with your right hand. Let me know when you've done it."

"I'm doing it, Doctor."

"Good. Now this is the part that she won't like. But you must do it if you want to fix her. Do you think you can?"

"I'm ready to try."

"Good. Now with your left arm holding Mandy's upper arm still, I now want you to pull steadily and strongly on her right wrist so that you're stretching her arm. Are you doing it?"

"I am. It doesn't seem to be bothering her too much."

"Good. Sometimes it does; sometimes it doesn't. Now you must do two things at the same time: maintaining tension on her arm all the while, I now want you to rotate Mandy's wrist to your left so her thumb faces out, and while you are doing that, I want you to bend her arm so that her hand comes up toward her shoulder. Did you do it?"

"Oh my god."

"What's wrong?"

"I felt something snap. I think I broke something. I heard a pop."

"You did. Good. You fixed it. The pop you heard was the elbow going back into place. Looks like we'll have to give you a degree in medicine. Congratulations."

"But she's still not moving it."

"Don't worry. She will. It may take a short while. Tell you what—I'll stay on the phone a few minutes. Why don't you just hold her left arm still and offer Mandy something she really likes, urging her to reach for it with her right hand."

(Doubtfully) "OK." *(After a few minutes)* "OK. She seems OK now. She's moving it. Thank you, Doctor."

"Don't mention it. Good job. Now let's see if we can all go back to sleep. There's nothing more for you to do."

There are few problems like this in medicine. The problem appears to be serious and arises suddenly; the diagnosis is generally easy, as is the treatment; and the cure is instant, or near instant—leaving the patient and parent happy. An office visit from a child with a dislocated radial head (nursemaid's elbow) provides a very bright light on a pediatrician's darkest day.

Darren–A Boy with Leukemia

For a pediatrician, there is, perhaps, no task more daunting than caring for a child with a potentially fatal illness. I first saw Darren when he was six years old. His mother brought him in to see me for bruising on his legs and trunk, and for easy tiring, which was unusual in his case since he ordinarily was so active.

Other than the bruising, the physical examination showed Darren to be quite pale. His liver and spleen were enlarged to palpation and appeared somewhat tender during the examination. Darren's blood count showed disturbingly high numbers of white blood cells, a lack of platelets, and a profound anemia (to explain his pallor)—all suggestive of leukemia.

I told Darren's mother he would have to be admitted to the hospital for more testing. I was almost certain I knew the diagnosis, but I did not want to say anything until I was absolutely positive. So when the mother asked what he had, I said something like, "We don't have all the test results yet, and I want to be absolutely sure you get the best information. When we have all the results, what I want to do is to arrange a family conference so we can sit down and discuss it. In the meantime, you might like to decide with your husband who should be at that conference. Siblings? A grandparent? etc."

A bone marrow test in the hospital confirmed our suspicions, and I arranged to have a conference with the family prior to Darren's discharge. The conference was arranged to allow adequate time for explanations and to answer questions, and it was set up so there would be no phone calls or other interruptions.

As with many chronic or potentially life-threatening illnesses, the assessment of the family begins before the conference starts and the first word is spoken. Sometimes we learn most from nonverbal communications: Who did the parents invite to the conference? Where did they sit? Were they next to each other? Did one literally lean on the other, or were the parents on opposite ends of the room? Who asked most of the questions?

In my experience there is no easy way to give the news I had to give. The conference opened with a statement that went something like this, "I know you've been worried about Darren. So were we. Well, we've done all the tests, and we have the results. We've consulted with everybody at the hospital, and I now think we can say, with certainty, Darren has leukemia." I remained silent afterwards, giving the statement time to sink in and waiting for a reaction from the family.

After stating the diagnosis, although the family had already done some considerable worrying about leukemia—in fact, suspected it, I knew that little was heard in the ensuing period. I knew it through similar experiences I had with other families after I delivered grave news to them such as I had just delivered. I knew it after non sequitur statements in our conference, and I knew it when a question was asked over something I might have explained many times before. Nevertheless, I spent a long time with the family in that conference. That time spent, although poor in communicating information, went far to reinforce feelings in the family that Darren's doctor was concerned and would be available to them.

It's a common thing with illness. I've seen it again and again. People feel illness comes as a punishment. After a child gets sick, parents have communicated to me on many occasions, "What did I do to deserve this?" So early on in the conference (and, as it happened, many times thereafter) I said, "I want you to know—it's important for you to know this—Darren's illness was no one's fault. Not yours, not his. It just happened, and nothing you could have done any sooner would have prevented it from happening."

I went on to explain the nature of leukemia, the drugs used and their side effects, allowing as much time as needed for questions. I tried being as forthright and honest as I could without creating alarm.

We discussed who should know about Darren's illness. The parents wanted to hide the fact of Darren's leukemia from his ten-year-old brother, grandmother, school teacher, and from Darren himself. It's hard to keep such a diagnosis secret. The medications Darren was taking would tip off a pharmacist who might be a neighbor, so I had his parents buy his medications in another neighborhood. The family would still have to explain frequent absences from school and the possibilities of hair loss. Had Darren been older, it would have been a real problem to keep the diagnosis secret from him. Children can be very perceptive. In cases where the parents try to hide the facts of the illness from the child, the child often comes to know. When the child doesn't want the parent to know he knows, both the child and his parents are hiding a secret that is with them all the time, and this puts a heavy strain on their relationship, preventing that very relationship from being the source of strength it can and must be.

One of the most difficult things about leukemia is its periodicity. There were times, when Darren was in relapse, when it was clear he was truly sick. However, there were other times, when Darren had responded to his treatments, or the disease was in a quiescent phase, when Darren was in remission. At those times, he was like any other child his age, and it was hard to imagine he was sick. During those "well" periods I often heard from his mother who wanted to know if we were sure of the diagnosis.

And, of course, I heard from Darren's mother when he was in relapse. She called me at all times: at the office during busy periods, in the still of the night, and on holidays. The calls, on those occasions, concerned weakness, pallor, fatigue, bruising, frank bleeding or fever—direct effects of the leukemia; or nausea, vomiting and/or ulcerations in the mouth—more often effects of the therapy. The calls became more frequent as the disease progressed and were soon tinged with anger—anger out of the parents' mounting concern for their child and growing frustration over not being able to do more for him—anger subsequently displaced to his physician.

For me, a difficult part of taking care of Darren was to "absorb" the blame placed on me by his parents. Were I to have removed myself as a target for blame, the parents would have been left with no one to blame but themselves for the course of his illness. Long after he would be gone and I would be out of the picture, the parents would be left with the task of living with themselves and questioning what more they could have done.

Darren continued to deteriorate despite all our best efforts and the benefits of excellent hospital care, and he finally died. As I look back on Darren's leukemia, I'm struck with a profound sadness. There has been a great deal of progress in medicine in the area of leukemia. The truth of the matter is acute lymphoblastic leukemia, the kind Darren had, is now often curable. Had Darren been born but a few years later, he might well have been cured, and I wouldn't be writing this story about him now.

Little Lillie

Lillie was cute as a button (and not much bigger.) At three years of age, she stood thirty inches tall and weighed a whopping twenty-four pounds, putting her at the third percentile in height and weight for girls her age.[4] When a child is below the third percentile of height and weight, and failing to keep up with the normal growth rate, we say that child has failure to thrive.

The one thing that differentiates pediatrics from other fields of medicine is that in pediatrics everything is examined against a backdrop of change—and that change is growth and development. The sine qua non of childhood is growth and development, and failure to grow can be caused by almost any problem in the entire spectrum of childhood illness.

---

[4] Third percentile in height means that for every one hundred children of Lillie's age, she would be taller than three and shorter than ninety-seven.

Other than being smaller than almost anybody, Lilly was a perfectly normal child. She was healthy, very active, pretty, and well-proportioned. I saw her in my office for well checkups only as she was never sick. Each time, she was brought in by her nanny (both her mother and father worked.) At each visit, she was weighed and measured, then her height and weight were plotted on a growth chart so I could measure her growth rate as well as her size against others her age.

Lilly fit the definition of a child with failure to thrive, and I had been watching her over a few office visits to see if she might enter into a growth spurt. I put off admitting her into the hospital hoping she'd sprout. But to no avail. Finally, my patience ran out. I told Lillie's nanny Lillie would have to be admitted to the hospital to determine why she wasn't growing and asked the nanny to have Lillie's parents call me so we could arrange for an admission.

At various times, I had reviewed Lillie's chart—her prenatal history, birth history, review of systems, and many physical examinations. With the aid of her parents I hoped to construct a better growth history including the heights, weights, and patterns of growth of her parents, grandparents, and siblings. I considered a reasonable approach to determine the cause of Lillie's growth failure, weighing the pros and cons of various tests and procedures with their likely yield against their cost, and I made up a plan for her hospitalization.

This case came to an unexpectedly premature resolution when Lillie's parents to came to the office. One look at them, and my face turned red as a beet. I could see they both came from a long line of short people the very moment they entered my office. Neither one of them was over five feet tall.[5]

---

[5] Needless to say, they were not charged for the office visit.

The Turkey

I had my internship and residency training at a county hospital. We saw, for the most part, patients who were sick and indigent, some of them without homes, or doctors of their own, whose concept of medicine meant end-stage care, and who almost always found their way into the hospital by way of the emergency room.

I was working on a ward that housed adults and children. I was working thirty-six hours on, twelve hours off. There were eighteen patients on the ward—twelve of them were dying. There was never enough time. Like so many other doctors in training at that time, I walked the wards in a state of limbo, like a zombie, somewhat dulled by a pervasive fatigue while at the same time stimulated by urgent needs and the reality of so many things to do and so little time.

As I recall, it was 3:00 or 4:00 a.m. I had just finished all my work on the ward, returned to the on-call room, undressed to my shorts, and snuggled into bed. I must have been sleeping but a few minutes when the telephone rang. I picked up the phone and put it to my ear—waiting for the cobwebs to clear out of my brain. "Hey," came a voice from the other end of the phone. "Whatcha doin'?" If I really had all my wits about me, I would have answered, "I was just lying here in bed waiting for your call," but I merely stated I had just got to bed and was looking forward to squeezing in a few hours of sleep. The call was from John, a fellow intern, who was working in the emergency room. John continued, "Hey, sorry to tell you this, but we're admitting a patient from the ER. Wait till you see him. He's a real turkey. We're sending him up with his X rays."

Needless to say, I was upset. A "turkey," in our language, meant someone who really didn't belong in the hospital, usually someone looking for a place to sleep, a meal, or needing social services. At 4:00 a.m., without seeing him, I was convinced he not only didn't belong in the hospital—I was certain he didn't deserve to be on the planet.

I struggled into my working togs and dragged myself over to the ward as I seriously considered if it wasn't too late for a change in careers. As I arrived on the ward, the patient was being wheeled up on a stretcher. From a distance the patient appeared to be a small child who was completely covered with blankets. Ordinarily, when a child was admitted to the ward, he arrived accompanied by his parents. There were no parents with him. His X rays stuck out from the stretcher. I quickly grabbed the films and walked over to a viewing box.

I was flabbergasted. When I looked at the films, I realized they were unlike any I'd ever seen before. The bones were far too thin; the sternum, prominent; and the ribs flared outward and curved posteriorly, leaving the chest, in a way, so misshapened one had to wonder how any air could have been exchanged in the process of breathing at all. This was no **turkey!**

I walked back to the cart and pulled the covers back from the patient.

It **was** a turkey. A twenty-four-pound turkey resting between two pillows. It was a hell of a trick to play on a fellow intern. And on Thanksgiving, too.

A Really Bad Day

It was a lousy day—one of those really bad days. Screaming kids. No cures. I didn't feel good. Felt like I was coming down with something and was getting worse as the day went on. I started early in the morning. Worked nonstop. Missed lunch. It was almost 6 p.m. I'd been behind almost the whole day. The parents were angry because they had to wait so long. I couldn't wait to get home. I was dog tired.

"Any more patients?" I asked the girls in our front office. "Your last one's going into a room right now," was the reply. I breathed a sigh of relief. I was more than ready to go home. I entered my room to see my last patients.

I felt discriminated against. Two of my associates were working in the office with me. They were not so busy, perhaps because I was the most senior in the practice; perhaps because it just so happened more of my patients had appointments and got sick that day. At the end of my last appointment, I sat at the desk and finished making my notes in the chart. I was so tired I could barely think straight. I looked out an open door across the hall and I saw a young couple through an open door sitting in one of my rooms.

I picked up the telephone and spoke over the intercom to the front office. I spoke loudly, not caring if anyone could hear—so that the couple across the hall could hear. "I thought you told me I was seeing my last patient of the day. You just gave me another. Look, I'm really beat. You know how busy I've been all day. Give them to someone else . . . . You can't? Why not?" The gentleman across the hall had made it very clear he wanted to see me and no one else. "No, he didn't have an appointment. I slammed the phone in the cradle and dragged myself across the hall.

Entering the room, the young man rose to greet me. He was smiling and extended his hand. Though I was certain he heard my phone conversation, it did not seem to bother him. "Dr. Aronson," he said. Remember me?" I didn't. And was in no mood for guessing games. "I'm Vito," he continued. "Vito Santucci. You saved my life!"

Vito went on to explain I had taken care of him some twenty-five years earlier when he was seven years old. On one occasion, he was rushed to our office with a severe attack of asthma. Apparently he made a dramatic recovery in our office, and his parents, and therefore Vito, were convinced it was due to my treatment. Therefore, I saved his life. Shortly after that visit, the family relocated, and I hadn't seen Vito in twenty-five years.

At that moment, I didn't remember Vito's illness. I stated that I seriously doubted I saved his life. I had only the barest recollection of Vito.

Vito had married and settled in a community located about thirty miles from our office. "This is my wife Adrien," he said. "I wanted her to meet the doctor who saved my life." Though it was a one-hour drive through heavy traffic from his house to our office, he explained he had long wanted to say hello. He thought he'd surprise me with a visit, was sorry he arrived so late, but not knowing we'd moved he first went to my old office and then had to find the new one. He showed me old pictures of him and his parents and we settled into an easy conversation that lasted far longer than I intended it to. After the visit, I felt more alive than I did when I arrived at the office in the morning.

It had really been a lousy day. One of those bad days. But then, at the end, I heard four words, "You saved my life." Suddenly, I couldn't remember why it had been such a bad day after all. It's days like that that made my work worthwhile.

Language

I studied Spanish my first two years of college, and I've tried to use it every opportunity that presented itself—not always without incident. I remember once talking to a young Spanish girl who blushed for some reason. I asked her if she was *embarasada*. It turned out I was asking her if she was pregnant.

I've made other mistakes too, trying to communicate in a language that was not truly my own. Not knowing the Spanish word for soap, I once told a mother, "Lave su bebe con sopa," in fact saying, "Wash your baby with soup." I got some strange looks for that one.

But language errors are not necessarily bad, or bad for business. In another instance, I mistakenly substituted the word *pollo* (chicken) for *polvo* (powder) saying, "Ponga un pollo en el cuello," which translated to "Put a chicken on the neck." The mother took me seriously, perhaps thinking I was advocating an *old home remedy,* her child improved, and she recommended three families to me.

On a more serious note it's obvious that little is learned unless we speak the same language. A teacher once told me she had trouble teaching a student to multiply. The student just couldn't seem to get the idea of "carrying over." After trying everything, in a final act of desperation, the teacher turned the job over to another student in the class. By the very next day the problem was solved. The appointed teacher simply told the problem student, "Six times four is twenty-four. You put the four down here and **tote** the two over here." The other student simply didn't understand the word *carry.* It wasn't part of his language.

My experience using a foreign language has been that people appreciated it when I tried to speak their language. It was an indication I respected them, and where they came from, and that I wanted to be sure they understood. On the other hand, it's most important for people from other countries to speak our language, so I encourage my patients to see to it that their children maintain the language of their heritage, while at the same time emphasizing they know English.

In some instances children growing up in bilingual, or multilingual homes start speaking later, but it doesn't look like their language suffers. Children learn languages very quickly—and dialects too. Their ears are very sharply attuned. I had a four-year-old patient who went to the southern United States on a two-week trip and returned speaking with a southern accent. After another few weeks, the accent was gone.

Language plays a very important role in diagnostic interviews, taking medical histories, and in consultations. In these areas other forms of language are important, e.g., pauses, words left unsaid, facial expressions, body posturing, and attitude. This is the **art** of medicine, skills we were never taught in medical school.

Handwriting

My father used to joke that whenever I wrote a letter home he had to take it to a pharmacist to have it read. Doctors have poor handwriting, it's a widespread belief, and when a belief is so popular there's usually some element of truth to it. Here's a story that supports that thesis.

A cousin of mine referred a young lady to me who was adopting a baby from China. The young lady called to know if I would take care of her baby and if there was any information I might need prior to her coming to our office. She would be leaving for China to see the baby for the first time and to bring it home to the United States.

I advised it would be best if she could obtain, before her trip to China, the complete medical records, including the history and health status of the baby's mother, the birth history, knowledge of any infectious diseases the mother had prior to delivery or the baby had after, significant family history of illness in the mother and baby's father—if known, all tests performed on the baby, and any shots or immunizations the baby might have received.

Not long thereafter I received a large packet of all the information I requested. The information was in Chinese.

A Caucasian friend who brought his children to my office was fluent in Chinese. He agreed to go over the medical reports with me, which he did. But although reports were understandable generally, there were parts where the writing was so obscure, it was undecipherable. So we showed the reports to my friend's wife who was Chinese. But she couldn't read them either.

I was jolted with the impact of a suddenly perceived universal truth. A doctor's handwriting is unreadable, whether it's in English cursive, Japanese or Chinese kanji, Arabic script, or Sanskrit.

Shots

Kids don't like shots. In the hallways of our office, before a foot is put in the door, one often hears, "I don't want a shot!" "Not the needle." "No shot, OK?" "You promised, no shot." "Do I need a shot?" "Pleeeease, no shots."

Though there's often some discomfort to a shot, it's clear to me a child's fear is out of proportion to it. At times, the parents don't help matters. I've heard some tell their children, "Be good, or I'll have the doctor give you a shot!"

Where there's fear in the parents the kids sense it as well. And, in fact, the fear of shots does extend to adults. I had a strapping teenage boy—a football player who could finish a game on a broken leg, who fainted on two separate occasions following shots—once for stitches, the other for a booster immunization. A father in our office once turned cold and clammy and fainted after I gave his son a shot. (I called the paramedics thinking, perhaps, he had a myocardial infarction or stroke, but he was fine.)

Pain itself intensifies the longer the child has to anticipate (or dread) the injection; and the longer the pain lasts following a shot, the stronger the memory of that last shot, and the more the child fears the next one.

I have never told a child a shot wouldn't hurt knowing, in fact, it would. That's a surefire way to destroy one's credibility. In my experience it's always better to say, "Now this will pinch just a little" and then give the shot as quickly as possible. If the child would say it hurt, I never argued, but rather I would say, "Of course, I told you so. I said it would pinch, didn't I? But it wasn't so bad—and you were really brave." Give the shot, apologize, and validate the pain.

Sometimes it's possible to give a shot so quickly the child hardly knows it—first by distracting him with a joke or by pointing to an object of interest, keeping the syringe and needle hidden, giving the shot quickly, and then hiding the needle and syringe so that the child never really knows what happened. A larger needle often hurts less than a smaller one because the shot is given more quickly—the exception being when a larger needle is used because the medicine injected is so thick. Some shots always hurt, probably because of the nature of the material injected, and some materials (such as long-acting penicillin) cause soreness at the injection site for a long period of time.

As far as immunizations go, despite the overwhelming data supporting the need for shots, there is, unfortunately, a counterculture led by a very small group of physicians that opposes them. Partly because shots do sometimes hurt, and partly because many of the diseases for which they are given are now rare (precisely because they have worked so well) there are a number of parents who oppose the idea of having their babies immunized, thus putting their children and others at risk, and for this reason all states require shots be given to all students as a prerequisite for attendance. In some cases where a family's religious beliefs prohibit immunizations, shots are withheld. Even in some of these families shots are sometimes given. (I had one family whose twenty-year-old daughter attended a university where two other unimmunized classmates had died in a measles epidemic.) That family ran (not walked) to our office to be sure their daughter was immunized.

There **are** risks to giving shots in medicine. But these risks are indeed small. It's important to understand that **all** procedures carry with them some risk, but when the risk of not doing them becomes far greater than the risk of doing them the procedures are done.

Burt

No sooner does the image of Burt come into focus—it fades. But memory is like that—strong and overpowering, persistent at times, then suddenly elusive and gone.

Burt was a patient I cared for thirty years ago. I can still picture him in my mind's eye, but if I was asked to describe him in detail I don't think I could. When I first saw Burt, he was four years old, and I was a pediatric intern (in my first year of training after medical school). He had been admitted to the hospital with a history of recurrent unexplained fevers, which had, for the first time, become associated with diarrhea, anemia, and rash. Burt was bright and talkative. His sandy hair stood up on the back of his head, and his brown eyes sparkled. He maintained a bravado and showed a stoicism beyond his age and size, covering his fears with an endearing smile. Burt soon recovered from his first hospitalization and was discharged without a specific diagnosis, but he was admitted several times thereafter with similar problems—each time a little sicker, each time slower to respond—but always cheerful, happy to see me, wanting to play, and looking forward to seeing old friends on the ward.

It was determined Burt had Wiskott-Aldrich Syndrome, a rare disease associated with frequent infections, diarrhea, rash, bleeding, and anemia. Burt and I had become great friends by the time the diagnosis was made. Because of this friendship, my role in his hospital care, and the fact that my wife and I were new in town, we became close friends of Burt's parents as well. They shared their concerns for Burt's health with my wife and me, and I supplied a sympathetic ear to their concerns and provided a sense of optimism born out of youth, inexperience, and a kind of naive hope for Burt's future,

My reading early on told me Burt had a fatal illness, and I first withheld the information from his parents. I found it hard—no, impossible—to accept the diagnosis, and therefore I saw no reason, early on, to discuss the likelihood of his dying with his parents. I remember his parents' disappointments and growing fears with subsequent hospitalizations. The illness was showing its effect on Burt also. Each time he entered the hospital he appeared less happy and energetic. His smile lost its luster; his eyes, their twinkle; and he became disinterested in play.

There were more and more medical questions that sent me to the library and philosophical questions I couldn't answer. Over the course of his illness there were tears my wife and I shed between us, and tears we shed together with Burt's parents. There was the unbearable weight of sadness when it became obvious his end was near—and finally, the grief of his death.

This was my first experience with the death of a young patient. I recall, beyond the sadness, those feelings I had as Burt's physician—feelings of inadequacy and betrayal. I believed the medicine I had learned would cure him—and I felt, in turn, my sense of optimism communicated this to his parents—in the end betraying the trust they placed in me as his doctor. Thirty-five years later now, I think I see it in perspective. One does the best one can do. It's just not always good enough. And sometimes there aren't answers—only questions.

Perspective, in life as well as art, makes things appear smaller and dimmer as they appear in the distance. But first experiences, though most distant, often carry the strongest impact. For the most part, Burt's features have lost their distinctness and clarity with time, but the impact of his death is poignant—perhaps even more palpable, and I think I'll carry it with me forever.

Byron and Bryon

Twins intrigue me. Some, though born of the same parents, in the same place, and at the same time, and raised in the same environment, end up as different as night and day; others look like peas in a pod (identical) and may be identical in behavior and temperament—even when they are separated at birth. Each twin is an individual, no matter how close he/she started on the astrological table and each occupies its own universe through life. And so we employ all means to separate the one twin from its counterpart by name, appearance, and sometimes even location. I heard of one mother with triplets. Keeping them straight was a constant challenge. Every morning she'd round them up and ask, "Now, who're you? And who're you?" She'd dress them so that she could identify each (so-and-so goes in red, so-and so in blue, so-and-so in green) and she'd put them in certain places with the admonition, half-desperate, "don't move!" so she could distinguish one from the other.

Imagine my confusion when I saw for the first time in my office, Byron and Bryon, twins of eight months, who were so close in appearance you couldn't tell them apart.

Our customary office procedure for new patients began with a detailed medical and social history and was followed by a physical examination and finally, laboratory tests, immunizations, and/or other treatments as needed.

I questioned Bryon's mother as to his medical history, and growth and development as she undressed him. Bryon had been placed on the examining table and I proceeded to give him a thorough examination. The phone rang at the end of his examination, an event that occurs not infrequently in our office. As I turned my attention to the call, Bryon was dressed and Byron undressed. When I turned around to face the table once more, I said, "OK, now let's dress this one and undress the other." And that's just what the mother did. I took the second chart, asking once again all the same questions and, of course, got the same answers. As I performed the second physical examination, I couldn't help but notice how much alike the twins were in every detail. After finishing the exam, I then said to the mother, "OK, you can dress the baby now."

On the way out of the office the mother asked, "How come you examined the same child twice?"

LaToya and Bill–Diabetes

If a pediatrician does a good job treating a child with diabetes, he just about puts himself out of business. The primary goals of treating the disease are optimal growth, minimal complications through good control of blood sugar levels, and education of the patient so that he becomes independent in the day-to-day management of the disease.

The challenges of managing diabetes are magnified in children for a variety of reasons:

1. Since the child is often too young to understand, many of the responsibilities for care are extended to others in the family.

2. The disease itself is different in children, almost always requiring insulin injections as well as closer monitoring of blood sugar levels, diet, activity, etc.

3. Changing levels of hormones associated with growth effect the course of the diabetes.

4. Various stages of development carry with them specific psychological stresses—e.g., a teenager, who wants to be like all his peers, may rebel against the need to follow a diabetic diet or to take insulin shots.

A case in point was LaToya. LaToya was a sixteen-year-old girl whose diabetes I managed when I was in training in Cleveland. She lived at home with her mother who was single and in constant battle with her daughter. LaToya had what we call a brittle form of diabetes, which found her with frequent bouts of hypoglycemia when she refused to eat or took too much insulin. These episodes of hypoglycemia caused sudden weakness, dizziness, and fainting spells that led to seizures. On other occasions, LaToya showed hyperglycemia associated with a huge increase in appetite, and excessive drinking, and urinating, which resulted in hospitalization for severe dehydration leading to coma. Blood tests performed on those admissions found LaToya near death from a metabolic ketoacidosis brought on by her neglected treatment. Invariably, following an argument with her mother, LaToya simply skipped giving herself insulin injections and went off her diet. Over a period of three months, LaToya was admitted on five separate occasions, near death, in this game of metabolic brinksmanship she was playing with her mother.

Appropriate medical care restored LaToya to balance and diabetic control, but in her case the most difficult thing was to convince LaToya and her mother how a miscalculation or delay could be fatal. A referral was made to family therapy where the mother/daughter relationship could get the psychiatric attention it so needed, and LaToya was placed in a foster home until it was felt she could safely return to live with her mother.

The experience was a dramatic lesson in addressing the psychological needs of the adolescent diabetic.

I served as a doctor on a six-week elective rotation at a camp for diabetic children during my training. Imagine, seventy-five adolescent diabetics over an extended period, all in the same place and at the same time. In such an arrangement diets are regulated, activities planned, and insulin doses determined on a daily basis, so one would expect the management of diabetes to have been easy. Surprise, surprise. It wasn't. There were things we had no control over.

One evening we found the blood sugars of all the campers in one cabin surprisingly elevated. At first, we wondered if a box of chocolates or some other caloric no-no found its way into the cabin. The campers denied any snacking, and a search of the cabin failed to turn up anything to explain the elevation of the blood sugars. What we did learn on further questioning was that the counselor for the cabin, who was a diabetic, and somewhat unstable at that, decided, that day, to teach his campers something. He caught some frogs, then sat his campers in a circle inside the cabin, put the frogs in the center of the circle and gave them intraperitoneal injections of insulin. In this way the counselor and the campers watched the frogs convulse and die in the middle of the cabin. I knew what went into the belly of the frogs, but I had no idea what went into the minds of the campers as a result of that episode. One can't help but wonder about the long-term consequences of such a prank. I tell the story only to illustrate how difficult it is to account for what enters the minds of these children.

There was another diabetic counselor at the camp. His name was Bill, but it should have been Sherman because he was built like a tank—a Sherman tank. Bill was wide and solid; about five feet eight inches tall and two hundred twenty pounds—all muscle. This created quite a problem for the rest of us on the camp staff, for every morning we found Bill unconscious in his cabin. Not sleeping; unconscious. It was dangerous to attempt to wake him. When aroused, he lashed out with his arms. To be standing too close meant to risk getting hit by a branch of a redwood tree. We determined Bill was overdosed from insulin when we found him in the morning, and we developed a safe way to bring him out of his state. Every morning six of us entered his cabin, pounced on him, and immobilized him, then squirted a glucose gel into his mouth between his cheek and his molars. It was crude and rough, but it worked. The effect of this was to raise his blood sugar. Shortly thereafter he could be safely awakened, and the rest of the day he was fine.

Bill was asked many times if he had been giving himself extra insulin shots and his response was always in the negative. He was taken into town to have blood tests run in a local hospital, but the test results all came back normal. The cause of Bill's hypoglycemic attacks remained a mystery until an empty box of insulin syringes and an empty vial of insulin was found at the edge of the woods not too far from his cabin. When confronted with the evidence, Bill, who received his daily shots from the dispensary like the other campers, admitted he had been giving himself extra doses. But he never told us why; perhaps he didn't know himself.

The Bills and LaToyas of this world teach us that when it comes to caring for the adolescent diabetic, educating the patient alone may not be enough for the doctor to "put himself out of business." Psychological wellness too is a requirement so that the patient can be depended upon to take the responsibility for his/her care. Fortunately, for every one like Bill or LaToya there are, perhaps, a vast majority who pass through adolescence without problems, who have learned to manage themselves and their disease, and who grow up without complications.

Pattie was a young diabetic girl who I had as a patient. She found her disease so interesting she went on to medical school. Phil had diabetes when he was quite young. I took care of him for many years. He walked into the office the other day with his two children.

Serendipity

When a thing happens by serendipity, that means it happens by chance. Sometimes the most gratifying things that happen to us occur by serendipity. Here's one of the highpoints of my life as a pediatrician, which has led to a lasting friendship and continues to reward me to this day.

About twelve years ago our daughter was returning from a visit with her sister who was living in Denmark. She was flying on Romanian Airlines. On her trip home she struck up a conversation with a young Romanian man who was coming to the United States to study for an advanced degree in computer sciences. He was leaving his pregnant wife in Romania to study at the University of Missouri in Rolla—ironically, a city in which we had cousins.

The young man, who we shall call Nikolai, had relatives who lived in the Chicago area, but he couldn't reach them. Our daughter suggested he accompany her to our home for coffee and conversation. Nikolai spoke quite acceptable English, which, it turned out, he had learned from reading spy novels. Before he left our house to continue on his trip, we gave him our cousins' phone number in Rolla in the event it would help him in settling in our country.

About two weeks after his arrival, Nikolai called our daughter. "What a country," he said. "I've been here only two weeks and already I've got an apartment, a telephone, a car, and a driver's license. I thought that would take me at least six months."

Our daughter informed him her luggage was missing from the flight, had been for two weeks, and that when she called Romanian Airlines they told her, "Two weeks? That's nothing. It usually takes at least six to find lost luggage."

A few days later, Nikolai called us. His baby boy had been born and was doing fine, except, as he understood it, the baby had a little sack hanging from his back and the doctors said he would need an operation in six to eight weeks.

It sounded to me like the baby had spina bifida, a congenital condition where the spinal cord ends outside the body in a blind sack. Such children are considered medical emergencies in our country and operated on as soon as possible to prevent infections such as meningitis, paralysis, hydrocephalus, and even death.

I told Nikolai to have his wife (who was a pediatrician in Romania) take pictures of the sack up close and from all directions, measure the baby's head on a daily basis, and to send the information to me.

When the pictures and serial measurements arrived, I then took them to the neurosurgeons of a fine hospital in Chicago. They, like me, felt surgery should be done as soon as possible, and offered to do it **pro bono**. We then talked to the director of the hospital, explaining that the pictures suggested adequate skin for a good closure, and that an uncomplicated surgery with potentially good results was possible. The hospital offered free treatment and board for the baby, and Nikolai and his wife made quick arrangements to come to Chicago.

Nikolai and his wife were our houseguests during the baby's (little Nikolai's) post-operative care. The surgery itself was quite successful, and after two sleepless nights for the parents it looked as if all might be well. I examined little Nikolai along with the neurosurgeons and viewed the post-surgical films with the radiologists. I was, and still am, in awe of what modern American medicine had to offer.

Little Nikolai now walks, runs, and has complete control of his excretory functions. He's bright and interested in everything. He's an avid soccer player and still literally springs out of his house on game days even though, to this date, his team has not yet won a game, or even scored a goal. Little Nikolai lives near Washington, D.C. and since we have often travelled there to see our daughter, we've visited him. At five or six, he'd often ask me questions like, "Hey Neil, how's Chicago going?" At seven, he asked if I knew Michael Jordan.

At eight or nine, he wanted to know the difference between Democrats and Republicans as well as who we voted for.

As I look at little Nikolai, whose miraculous recovery, I feel, resulted though a blend of modern, high quality medical care and caring, I fully realize how serendipity made it all possible, and I'm grateful each time I see my precious little friend.

Occupational Hazards

Tommy's eyes glistened with a mischievous twinkle. Had I only been a little more sensitive I might have picked up the predatory intensity in them too. When I entered the office, he was ready for me. I'd seen Tommy many times before. He was a surly and unpredictable kid, so when he rushed forward to meet me I stood guard, but perhaps I wasn't guarded enough. Little did I know that something was afoot.

In the tradition of Pele, the greatest soccer player of them all, and with the strength of a fifty-yard field goal, Tommy gave me a kick. In the shins. Ohhh, did it hurt!

To my surprise, Tommy's mother laughed—a high-pitched, nervous laugh. I, on the other hand, fumed. I was angry, and my first impulse was physical retaliation. Tommy's mother's behavior hadn't help matters any. Her laughter was a bitter frosting on a very bitter cake. I limped to my desk and sat down. I had a brilliant idea! I took a routing slip and wrote the bill—then gave it to her.

Tommy's mother was no longer laughing. She took her son by the arm, then left my office, and then walked to the reception desk and paid her bill. Despite my anger, I felt a mild sense of guilt for charging her, but I suppose I looked at it as combat pay, and the pain I felt in my shin made the submission of a bill feel right. As I reflected on it later, I realize her laughter was the result of surprise and embarrassment.

Tommy returned to see me the following week for his previously scheduled routine visit. He was well-behaved—a Little Lord Fauntleroy. There was no discussion of his previous visit. I'm sure, for his mother, all that remained of that event was a vague memory. For me, all I had was a tender lump— and a limp.

Conversation between the Thumb and the Pacifier

THUMB: Babies love me.

PACIFIER: They can't get rid of you, even when they want to.

THUMB: They become attached to me. Because I'm always there for them. Even in the middle of the night.

PACIFIER: With me, kids get variety. I come in different sizes, shapes, and colors. Sometimes I'm plastic; sometimes I'm rubber.

THUMB: Not me. I'm flesh-colored. I'm natural. What you see is what you get.

PACIFIER: And sometimes what you get, from constant use, is a big growth on the knuckle.

THUMB: That's natural too. Anyhow, it goes away. You know, some mothers don't want their babies seen with you.

PACIFIER: And other mothers don't like the looks of their older kids when they're with you. Some kids keep you till they're ten years old. That's unsightly.

THUMB: They like me. They can't live without me.

PACIFIER: Not when their teeth jut out, or their mouths become crooked.

THUMB: I've seen it happen with you too.

PACIFIER: But with me I can be separated. As you yourself said, "You're attached." I tell you it's tragic.

THUMB: Well, I'll tell you one thing. When I come out in the middle of the night, the kid puts me back in; when you come out in the middle of the night, a parent gets up and puts you back in. I don't imagine that makes you too popular.

PACIFIER: Don't worry about me. I've got my fans. I get the job done.

THUMB: Me too.

PACIFIER: Let's face it. Those little suckers like us.

THUMB: You're right. With us, they're happy—and quiet. And when they're quiet, their parents happy.

BOTH: Three cheers for us. Rah, rah, rah!

Unintended Consequences

One day, I received a phone call from my friend Hank. "Neil," he said. "How ya doin'?" Hank never called me during the day, and I'd seen him only three nights earlier.

"I'm OK," I answered warily, thinking he was going to ask me for a favor.

"I want you to do me a favor," Hank said. He went on to tell me about a friend of his whose son went to Canada to escape the draft. His friend moved to Canada too and was living together with his son and other war protesters in a commune there.

They were all visiting in Chicago when the friend's son got sick and was taken to an emergency room. The son, who was very thin, had sickly yellow skin, hair that sprouted from his head in a spectacular afro, and was dressed in motley, along with his rag-taggle group of *communies*. They must have been quite a sight. It wasn't long before a squad of police were in the emergency room questioning the members of the commune (since, in the minds of many, anyone who looked like a hippie was thought to be on drugs). The son was found to have hepatitis, and it was recommended all in the commune get shots to prevent the illness, but the group, feeling they were being hassled by the police, fled the hospital. The father then called my friend Hank for a referral to a private physician for the shots, and Hank called me.

The father, who must have been in his midfifties, had been a successful investment counselor and had lived in a nice home on the North Shore of Chicago with his wife, son, and daughter. The Vietnam War deeply affected the son, and in fact, split up the family. So when the son fled to Canada to avoid the draft, the father gave up his beautiful home, and boat, and pristine lifestyle to go with him.

After hearing the story, I told Hank to tell the father that I would see the group in my office at the end of the day, and I volunteered to give them the shots.

The group came, but not at the end of the day. They arrived at about 3:00 p.m. It was a busy day. There were kids all over our waiting room: toddlers, preschoolers, primary graders, and older. Among the Canadian group, there were seven in number. There were six males and a rather attractive blond female, all of them looking like they were in their midtwenties, except for the father.

I was called to the front office when the group arrived and reassured them I would see them as soon as I could. I then returned to my examining rooms to see the patients who had been waiting.

Shortly thereafter I received a page, once more, from the reception desk. "Dr. Aronson," our receptionist said. "You'd better come up front." I could sense the urgency in her voice so, without asking why, I excused myself from an examining room and rushed up to the reception desk. There, as in the innocence of a summer picnic, and with the nonchalance and bliss of two lovers in a secret garden, the fifty-year-old was "making out" with his twenty-five-year-old chick in the center of our waiting room—in a manner that strained the bounds of privacy and propriety.

I had to do something—and quick! All my emergency room training, all the textbooks and lectures in pathology and biochemistry, infection and trauma, would be of no use to me now. I had to act with the speed of Mercury and the wisdom of Solomon. I couldn't help but think that medical school had not prepared me for this.

I led the group—lovers included—to a small lunch area we reserved for our employees in the back of the office. "Make yourselves comfortable here," I said—*but not too comfortable, I thought.* "I'll be back in a few minutes," I walked to our laboratory where we kept the injectables, quickly drew up the syringes, and returned to the lunch room to give the shots.

I then gave the bill to the father, suggesting he alone go to the front of the office to pay it while the others remain in the back. After the father returned, the group thanked me, and I ushered them out the back door telling them it would be best for them to leave that way so as not to interfere with our traffic flow (a lame excuse, but I had to say something, and it was the best I could come up with).

In a search for meaning I keep thinking there was a lesson to be learned in the whole episode. On the one hand, I had done what I had been trained to do as a physician—prevent disease, and I had performed a favor for a good friend. On the other hand, the whole experience exposed our little angels to some "visuals" that were not meant for their eyes, although, as I think back, the kids were, for the most part, oblivious to the tempestuous activities going on in our waiting room.

What I learned was a lesson in unintended consequences. We can't always avoid them, nor should we. They add an element of surprise and the challenge of adventure to our lives. I'm glad I gave those shots. Who said "Never volunteer for anything"?

I Love You, Mommy, I Love You, Daddy

I wish Mommy and Daddy wouldn't fight.

I love you, Mommy. I love you, Daddy.

They yell at each other behind the bedroom door.

I hear you, Mommy. I hear you, Daddy.

I hear my name. Did I do something wrong?

I'm sorry, Mommy. I'm sorry, Daddy.

Sometimes, after a fight, Mommy says something bad about Daddy.

Please, Mommy. Don't talk, Mommy. I love you, Daddy.

Daddy says something bad about Mommy.

Please, Daddy. Don't talk, Daddy. I love you, Mommy.

Sometimes, after a fight, Mommy and Daddy don't talk,

Please say something, Mommy. **Talk** *to me, Daddy.*

I want to say something, but I don't know what to say.

I'm scared, Mommy. I'm scared, Daddy.

Sometimes, after a fight, Mommy cries. Then I get mad at Daddy.

I hate you, Daddy. Don't cry, Mommy.

Then Mommy gives me a hug.

I love you, mommy.

Sometimes, after a fight, Daddy leaves. Then I get mad at Mommy.

I hate you, Mommy. Come back, Daddy.

When Daddy comes back, he sits me on his knee.

I love you, Daddy.

When Mommy and Daddy fight, I get angry; then I do something bad. I don't know why I do something bad.

I'm sorry, Mommy. I'm sorry, Daddy.

Sometimes I'm so sad I just cry. Daddy holds me.

Don't fight, Daddy. I love you, Daddy.

Mommy gives me a kiss.

Don't fight, Mommy. I love you, Mommy.

Mommy says, "I know you don't like us to fight. But sometimes we just can't help it."

I love you, Mommy.

Daddy says, "**You** don't make us fight. Sometimes it just happens."

I love you, Daddy.

Then Mommy and Daddy give me a kiss and hug me so tight. I know they'll love me forever.

I love you, Mommy. I love you, Daddy.

Friday the Thirteenth

I took care of Susan when she was a child; now she had three of her own. I saw them all in my office on Friday the thirteenth for checkups.

Susan had twins—Eric, a boy, and Lily, a girl who were nine months old—and Stacy, a daughter of four years. The twins were on the floor—in infant seats.

I first examined Lily, an examination that proceeded quietly and without incident. Lilly was put back in her infant seat.

Eric was undressed and put on the examining table. As I was finishing Eric's exam, a laboratory girl entered the room to draw bloods.

In the course of a physical, I usually examine the throat last. Babies don't like having their throats examined. It's a little thing called the "gag reflex." In the course of examining Eric's throat he gagged, and in doing so lunged forward so the tongue blade cut the back of his throat. I saw some bleeding, and so I told Susan what happened, that Eric was probably swallowing some blood, that a few drops of blood in the stomach could create a quantity of black liquid—which, if vomited, would look like a huge volume, But not to worry. The cut was minor, already the bleeding had almost subsided, and the cut would quickly heal without treatment.

Infants don't like having their fingers pricked. It's a little thing called pain, and the procedure added a few decibels to the serenity of the visit.

It was now time to examine Stacy the four-year-old sister. Stacy was a little lady, and her examination went smooth as silk. I learned it was Stacy's birthday and that she was going to have her ears pierced for a birthday present. Susan told me I had pierced her ears when she was four years old and asked if I would do Stacy's, and I agreed.

Ear piercing is not one of those things all pediatricians do, but I liked doing it for the following reasons:

1. It was one of those little extra services I could do for families, and it made the children and mothers happy.

2. I did it well—minimizing pain and the possibility of infection, and generally placing the earrings in the best spot.

3. It made our little girls look even prettier, leaving them, perhaps, with a pleasant reminder of their trip to the pediatrician.

Susan took great pains to make sure I knew exactly where she wanted me to place the earrings. The first earring went in well, and Stacy was pleasantly surprised that she felt no pain—something that made me quite happy since, when the first one is difficult, the second is often impossible. I then prepared the second ear, cleaning it thoroughly and marking the spot where the earring would go. Stacy was still and quiet. When I pierced the ear, I instantly saw the earring was too low. The piercing seemed to hurt Stacy, who was now squirming, somewhat and whimpering.

I told Susan the placement was poor and apologized—explaining that it happened infrequently and that it could be remedied right away by putting in another. By doing so, I explained, the first hole would close up instantly. Susan was reluctant to subject Stacy to another piercing, but she too was unhappy with the location and agreed to having it done again.

So once again I cleansed the ear and put in another earring. I don't know how it happened! Maybe Stacy had a momentary nervous twitch, perhaps I miscalculated, but whatever the cause this time the earring went in even lower—almost off the ear. This repiercing was even more painful leaving Stacy—and her mother—in tears.

Knowing that if I left the earring in place Susan would never be satisfied, I talked her into letting me do it one final time, and this time the earring was placed where it should have been in the first place. The beauty of the placement, however, was lost on Stacy, who was now hysterical.

At this point, the twins were screaming from having their fingers pricked, Stacy was hysterical from her multiple ear piercings, and Susan was crying in sympathy. The room had suddenly grown much smaller. Out of a sense of guilt or responsibility for having caused the commotion, and frustration for not being able to quell it, I wanted only to finish the office visit, which was the last scheduled one of the day.

Suddenly, the air was now pierced with a new even more terrifying sound. Not the cough of a cold, or even bronchitis, but the hacking, choking cough of a lodged chicken bone or the stridor of an end-stage croup. It was coming from Lilly!

Lilly had managed to pull the Band-Aid off her finger and aspirated it. It had become lodged in her windpipe. She had stopped breathing, and her face was turning blue. Now Susan too was hysterical! "Oh my god," she screamed, "What's happening to my baby? She's dying. She's dying!"

I too was dying—although my heart was racing. I picked up Lilly, from behind, wrapped my arms around her, and applied pressure—a procedure called the Heimlich Maneuver. The Band-Aid popped out.

The office now had six people in it: a nurse, one screaming baby, one recently near-dead blue baby, a hysterical multipierced four-year-old, a hysterical mother, and me—a precoronary pediatrician.

I was trembling. My throat was dry. And I was dazed. And crazed. It was Friday the thirteenth.

On Saturday the fourteenth I first thought about retirement.

Yitzie

Like most Saturdays, it was a very busy day. My schedule was completely filled. Anyone without an appointment would have to be squeezed in between scheduled visits.

"Why, hello, Yitzie," I said as I entered the next room. Yitzchak was standing alone in the examining room. "Where's your mother?"

"She doesn't know I'm here," he answered. Yitzie was eight years old and lived one block from our office. He had no appointment. "I just walked over." Yitzie looked down and shuffled his feet. He was wearing shiny black shoes, a striped shirt, solid vest, and tie. His sideburns hung down in long curls—not uncommon among young boys of his religious persuasion.

"When your mother finds out you're missing, she'll worry about you."

Yitzie moved his feet once again—then said, "It's OK."

"It must be something very important for you to come here on your own."

"It is," said Yitzie, breaking into an ear-to-ear grin.

"You don't look sick. Is there some problem you wanted to discuss with me?" "Not really," he stated. He looked at me directly, then asked, "Would you draw my picture?"

During our brief chat the phones were ringing continuously. There were busy sounds all around—doors opening and closing, voices, babies crying. The office was full. I was behind seeing my patients.

"This is Saturday, Yitzie. It's the busiest day here." I saw a look of disappointment in his face, but then I thought of something. "I can't do it now," I said, "but I'll tell you what. Why don't you go to the front desk and make an appointment for a portrait. I'll do it then, OK? I promise." (It was the first time anyone ever came to see me solely to get a portrait.)

"OK," he said

"Meanwhile, I think you better hurry back home. When your mother finds out you're missing, she'll worry about you."

As this portrait will attest, Yitzie did come back.

What's in a Name?

A man walks into a doctor's office and says, "I've got this problem, Doctor. I can't remember anything."

"Well," says the doctor, "let's look at your problem."

"What problem?" asks the man.

Having always had a good memory, I thought that joke was funny. Until I started forgetting names. Now it's not so funny anymore.

I had a partner who was very poor at remembering names, but he had a prodigious memory. He would say to me, "I saw that father of those patients of yours yesterday. He told me you really did a great job with his kids."

"Who is he?" I asked.

"You know," he'd say, "his left ear is bigger than his right, and he didn't pay his bill all last year until I talked to him. He has a boy and a girl."

As a pediatrician, forgetting names or events in a patient's history was understandable though particularly embarrassing. It occurred most often with older children who I had cared for over many years. And that's because most children, when they reached a certain age, began coming to the office less frequently—at a time when they changed most rapidly and dramatically. It got so, I was afraid to venture out into the community for fear of running into an older patient—one I had known for fifteen to twenty years, and that I didn't recognize. Naturally, of course, the patient and parent wouldn't have forgotten me. After all, I may have had twenty thousand visits in the interim, but the patient had only one pediatrician. At times, it would turn out I had performed a service that was relatively routine, or that I had forgotten, but which was of great impact or importance to the patient.

It's hard on the ego. My father-in-law, encountering a problem he never had before, asked me, "Have you ever had trouble remembering a name?" (At that time, he was ninety-one years old.)

Long ago I read a book entitled *Stop Forgetting,* but one day I forgot where I put it. I **do** remember that the book stated that the secret to remembering names and events lies in association. The trick is to associate a face with a familiar word, or a name with a picture, so that—if practiced enough—it becomes habit. So I practiced. But apparently not enough.

Sometimes I was so tired I couldn't concentrate; sometimes I forgot the name or face I was associating.

My wife and I devised a plan. If we ran into an old patient, my wife would approach the patient, or parent, and introduce herself. Then we had only to sit back and wait to hear them introduce themselves back.

Of course, I could have just said something like, "I'm sorry. Please forgive me. I'm blocking on your name." Since so many of us block, the *confessional approach* does fly, but I don't usually do that, and I'm sure that goes for most of us.

Just because I don't remember a name, it doesn't mean I don't remember the person. But I'm afraid it might look that way, and, in not remembering, be letting someone down.

What I do, more often, is bluff. I would pretend like I remembered, give an enthusiastic of-course-I-know-you-so-happy-to-see-you hi, and follow up with a "What's new? What are you doing now? How long has it been since you were in the office? My god, you look great." Or if I was really daring and in the mood for a closer approximation to honesty, "You've changed so much I hardly recognized you." Or perhaps, if I was in the mood for humor, "I hardly recognized you. By the way, who are you?"

Forgetting names is a problem common to so many of us. But it **is** a particularly difficult one for a pediatrician to cope with. After all, our relations with patients and their parents are serious, sometimes intense, and personal, and go on for many years. We often take on the role of another parent, and parents aren't supposed to forget their children. And even if the problem is more subjective than real, for us it's real enough, and it's our perception of its importance that matters.

I have a friend who used to joke about a song titled, "I'll Never Forget What's-Her-Name." Usually, when a thing is joked about enough—it's serious. And universal. So pardon me if the next time someone tells me a joke about memory, I don't laugh. Maybe I don't know how to. Or perhaps, I just forgot.

Conversations

Where are we going, Mommy?

To the doctor's.

Whose doctor? Your doctor or mine?

Your doctor, Tommy.

Doc A.?

Yes, of course. You know your doctor, Tommy.

I like Doc A.

I know you do.

Do you think he'll give me a shot?

I don't know, Tommy. We'll see when we get there.

I don't like shots.

I know you don't, Tommy.

Do you think he'll put that stick in my throat?

I don't know, Tommy. But you're brave. You can handle it.

I don't want to handle it. I don't think he's gonna put a stick in my throat. Do you think Doc A.'s gonna tell me a joke?

I suppose he will. He always does, you know.

I know. And it's always the same joke.

I think you'd be disappointed if it wasn't.

I bet he tells every kid that joke. Do you think they laugh when they hear it?

I imagine so, Tommy. If they didn't laugh, I don't think he'd tell it.

I don't always laugh when he tells me a joke. Doc A. is sure a good artist. Do you think he'll draw my picture?

He did before, Tommy.

I know. But again. Do you think he'll draw my picture again.

I don't know, Tommy. He's so busy. Why don't you ask him? I like it when he draws my picture. He gives me muscles, even bigger than Daddy's. Do doctors have muscles, Mommy?

Of course, Tommy. But more important than that, doctors have brains.

Do I have brains, Mommy?

I think so, Tommy.

What are brains, Mommy?

They help you think, Tommy. They help you understand things. If you didn't have brains, you wouldn't ask so many questions.

Do I ask many questions, Mommy?

Oh, boy.

Doc A. asks a lot of questions.

He wants to know how you're feeling, Tommy. That's his job to ask questions.

I thought being a doctor was his job.

It is. But asking questions is what doctors do when they're working.

And give shots, Mommy?

And give shots.

And draw pictures?

No, Tommy. All doctors don't draw pictures.

I like doctors who draw pictures—and tell jokes.

Those are good things, Tommy. But the most important thing is to keep you well and to make you well if you should happen to get sick. **That's** what a good doctor does.

I like Doc A. Do you, Mommy?

Yes, I do, Tommy.

More than Daddy?

I like Doc A. for your doctor, Tommy. And I like your father for your daddy.

You know what I'm gonna do when I see Doc A., Mommy?

No. What, Tommy?

I'm gonna ask him if he heard about that guy—you know, that guy who they had to take away the whole left side of his body. You know why, Mommy?

Why, Tommy?

'Cause then I can say, "He's all right now," before he says it to me. Do you think he'll get it, Mommy?

He'll get it, Tommy.

Can I be a doctor when I grow up, Mommy?

You can be whatever you want, if you work hard enough. But you'd have to go to school a long, long time if you wanted to be a doctor.

Five years?

More than that.

Fifty years? A million years?

Oh, probably not that long, Tommy.

I don't mind school. I like school. Do you know why, Mommy?

No. Why, Tommy?

My teacher gives me stickers.

Look, Tommy. We're here at Doc A.'s office.

Mother and Tommy are sitting in the examination room when Doc A. enters. Tommy jumps up and says, "Hey, Doc A. Did you hear about that guy—they had to remove the whole left side of his body?????"

A Stitch in Time

Vanessa
(after her stitches
are out)

Michael needs to have his stitches out.

Michael says, "Is it gonna hurt? Is it gonna hurt?"

"Not too much," I answer.

"That means it's gonna hurt, right?" he asks.

"Not really," I say. "Well, maybe just a pinch."

"I don't want my stitches out. You don't have to take them out. Why not just leave them in? OK?"

"We can't do that," I say. "You don't want a great big scar on your face, do you?"

"I don't mind scars, really. I like scars. I think it's gonna hurt, and I **don't** want my stitches out."

"We can't leave them in. You'll get an infection," I say.

"I've had infections before. Lots of times. They're not so bad. Pleeease don't take my stitches out," screams Michael.

I put on my most serious look, "Now listen, Michael," I say. "You just relax. Have I ever lied to you?"

Michael says, thoughtfully, "No."

"That's right," I say. "No, I've never lied to you. I promise you it won't be nearly as bad as you think. You've got to trust me. Be brave and relax. Now close your eyes."

Michael closes his eyes and grits his teeth. "OK."

The stitches come out easily. One, two, three, four, five. "That's it," I say.

"That's it? You mean, that's it?" Michael asks incredulously.

"That's what I said," I answer. "They're all out."

Michael opens up his eyes to see me collecting the forceps and scissors and throwing away a used gauze pad and some paper. He lets out a short staccato laugh, and an expression of sheer joy comes over his face.

"Gee, Doc," he says, "you're a real pro."

It's *Not* an Emergency!

The phone rings. Doctor?

Yes. This is the doctor.

My kid, Jakob. I take him to the emergency room?

Excuse me. Who is this?

Mr. Bashar. My kid, Jakob. He's eighteen months old. He's really sick. I take him to the emergency room?

What seems to be the problem?

He's got really high fever tonight.

Since when?

Tonight. It's almost 101, Doctor.

Does anything seem to bother him?

I don't know. He cries a lot. He's burning up. And he's got snuffles.

Is he crabby? Pardon?

Is he irritable? Is he crying a lot?

No. He's got snuffles. And he's burning.

What's he like? Is he happy? Playful? Does he respond?

He's play OK. He's good smiler. But he no breathe. He's too stuffy.

How's everyone else at home?

Everyone's got colds. Me too.

That's just what it sounds like. A cold. A virus. Look. There's no cure for that. But he'll get better. If he's fussy, a little Tylenol might help him. But not to worry. See how he does overnight; and if you're still worried about him in the morning, call the office and we'll take a look at him.

I'm taking him to the emergency room.

I'm sorry, but I really don't think that's necessary. It's not an emergency, and I can't approve it for your insurance.

I'm worried.

I understand your concern. But you'll have to trust my judgment on this. See how Jacob looks in the morning, and if you're still worried, call the office for an appointment.

I take him to emergency room, now.

I'm sorry, but I can't approve it for your insurance because it's not a true emergency.

I worried. I take him anyhow.

A few hours later, I received a call from the emergency room doctor. Jakob had just been seen. He was felt to have a cold and was about to be discharged. He was fever free at the time he was examined. I asked to be put on the phone with the father.

Your son has a cold. He should be better in a few days. If you have any problems or questions, you can call our office.

You not give him something, Doctor?

If he's too stuffy and can't sleep, we can try something to help him breathe. Otherwise, as I told you before, he'll really get better on his own. It's a viral infection.

He need antibiotic.[6] An antibiotic won't help him. What

---

[6] This is, perhaps, one of the most common misconceptions lay people have—that antibiotics cure colds. Requests for them are so frequent, and arguments over their need are so fervent, one is often tempted to just give them rather than

did the emergency doctor tell you? Emergency doctor say he don't need nothing. But I want you should give antibiotic.

I won't do that. It's not the best thing for your child. Apparently the emergency doctor didn't think so either. And he just finished examining him.

Emergency doctor tell me he not children doctor.

That's why I suggest you bring Jacob to our office in the morning if you're still worried about him.

Mr. Bashar slammed the phone in its cradle. The following morning, he stormed into our office. He was furious. He had spent three hours the previous night in an emergency room at a personal cost of two hundred dollars and his son had received no treatment.

Doctor Aronson?

Yes, I'm Dr. Aronson.

I never see you before. I always see Dr. Tucker.

That's OK. What can I do for you?

---

argue over the fact they're not needed. Indiscriminate use of antibiotics selects out resistant strains of bacteria increasing the growing problem of resistant bacteria in the community and enhances the likelihood that the patient might have an allergic reaction.

You not to send my boy to the emergency room last night.

Oh, yes, I remember. It wasn't an emergency. How is he this morning?

He sleeping.

I then explained to Mr. Bashar my strong feelings about the need to reserve the use of emergency rooms for true emergencies. This is to avoid the excessive waits and unavailability of help for those who really need it. My explanation, however, did not appear to register.

I want see your license.

Do you think I'd be practicing without a license?

Show me your license.

I showed Mr. Bashar my license. Afterward, he left my office in a huff. About one week later, the office received a letter from Mr. Bashar's HMO. The HMO stated it had received a letter from Mr. Bashar, which claimed I rendered poor care to his son, and they requested an explanation. I framed a reply, returned it to the insurance company, and never heard of that episode again.

I don't know why Mr. Bashar was so angry. I understand that in a profession where there are so many critical decisions made in a day, there are opportunities for error or misunderstanding. As a doctor, therefore, one is always open to unexpected confrontations. Parents call or visit our office, worried over the health of their children, often deprived of sleep and exasperated over long waits. They didn't expect to have to miss work, and they're often concerned over new unexpected expenses. This is not an ideal climate for human contact, but then, that's pediatrics.

A Trip to the Office

(From a Five-Year-Old's Point of View)

Kids are smarter than we give them credit for. But they don't always say what's on their minds. Not in so many words anyhow. I've had a long time to observe them and to hear what they do say, and what follows is what I think goes through the mind of a five-year-old on the occasion of his preschool visit.

Why does Mom look so nervous? She's been talking to me a lot this morning, moving around even more than usual. I heard her tell someone over the phone she was taking me to the doctor. Does she think I don't know? Didn't she hear me cry when we were within two blocks of the doctor's office?

The waiting room is packed with red-faced kids. Their noses are running. Some of the kids who are leaving are crying. *I'll bet they got shots.*

In the center of the waiting room floor is a pile of toys. A toddler wipes his nose on his sleeve; then wipes his sleeve on a toy. An infant crawls up to the toy, picks it up, and puts it into his mouth.

Mommy keeps talking to me. She hasn't talked this much to me at home. She talks to me about everything but what's going to happen when I get into the doctor's office. Does she think I don't know? The last time I got a shot, she cried. The doctor almost did too after I bit him. Near a pile of toys in the corner is a pile of books. The books look chewed. Nearby, a baby sits with a corner of a book in his mouth. Some of the books are ripped. One mother has her child on her lap and is actually reading to her.

Look at that boy. He's really busy. The little boy is running to various parts of the waiting room to hide a glove or hat or scarf. *His mother looks angry. She's looked like that ever since he emptied her purse on the floor.*

I know why they call this a waiting room. I'm bored.

Two women, sitting next to the five-year-old and his mother, are discussing their children's pediatrician. *He's not my doctor. I wonder if Mommy talks about my doctor with her friends. Their children's doctor sounds scary. When my doctor sees me, he usually smiles, makes some silly sounds as if I was a baby, tickles me and says "hoochy kootchy," and then gives me a shot. I know when he smiles it means, watch out! My doctor smiles all the time. Why not? He didn't get the shot. I hate that.*

The office is filled with all kinds of noises. The mother has finally put all her things back in her purse and gathered up the articles of clothing her son scattered throughout our waiting room. She grabs him by the arm and yanks him toward her. "You'll be the death of me yet," she says. "Now you sit right here or I'll have the doctor give you a shot." *She doesn't have to scream. I hate that. Look. That little girl lets her mother take off her hat and coat. Without a fight. Not me. When Mom tries to take off my hat and coat, I fight her. She thinks I'm fighting just to fight. She doesn't know I understand the more clothes I let her take off, the closer I know I am to getting a shot.*

*A nurse opens the door to the waiting room and calls out a name. It sounded like mine. Mommy picks me up and carries me through the door into the office. It **was** my name. What's your hurry, Mommy?*

I know what happens now. I'm going to be undressed and placed on a scale. Mom's going to be surprised to learn I've gained weight—more than she expected. It's funny she's so happy, because I hear her talking with her friends, and they all pretty much want to lose weight. Maybe I'll understand when I get older.

I'm now completely undressed. My hands and feet are cold. The table I'm lying on is cold. I've got goose bumps. The doctor is asking Mommy so many questions about me—like he's really interested in me and cares about me. If he cares so much about me, why is he smiling while I'm lying on this cold table without any clothes on? Will it hurt less if I get a shot while I'm freezing?

The doctor picks me up and turns me this way and that. He sets me on my back, feels my stomach, and listens to my heart. He examines my ears.

Uh-uh, now he's going to look in my throat. Oh no, not that stick. I know he's going to tell me it won't take long and not to choke. Does he think I'm choking because I want to?

The examination is over. If the exam is over, how come I'm not being dressed? It looks like Mommy and the doctor are waiting for something. Can it be? Oh no, they must be waiting to give me a shot.

"Let's go, Mommy," I say. "Let's go," I tell her, pulling at her sleeve. "We're all done." I turn to the doctor. "Byyyeee!" I say, "We're going home now."

Here comes the nurse. She's got something in her hands. She's trying to hide something from me. "What are those?" I ask. "Am I gonna get a shot? I don't want a shot. No shots, Mommy, right? Doctor, are you going to give me a shot?" *My doctor keeps smiling. Does he enjoy this?*

"I'm not going to go to school," I say. *If I don't go to school, I won't need a shot. Now the doctor's laughing.* "I hate you, Doctor. You're mean. I'm never coming here again."

Children's Picture Books

Children love stories about animals—especially dragons. "Bobo the Dragon" is a story about how one creature, against all odds, succeeds through great determination and with the help of a few good books.

Bobo The Dragon

Bobo the Dragon wanted, from birth,
To be a fireman, the best one on earth.
There was no question he had the desire.
His heart beat with purpose; his eyes burned with fire.
So lickety split to the firehouse he sped
Where he asked for a job, and the fire chief said,
"It's clear to see, Bobo, desire you've got
But a dragon can't be what a dragon is not.
For everyone knows—and there is no doubt
That a dragon starts fires; he does not put them out."
Was poor Bobo beat? Did he think he would never
Get to be Bobo the best fireman ever?
Not Bobo, oh no, for he burned with desire
And one just doesn't put out a true dragon's fire.
So Bobo practiced the firefighter things
He could do with his tail; he could do with his wings.
And he read about fires so he could then show
There wasn't a thing that he didn't know.
He read books about all the great firemen of yore
He read stories of fires. He read stories galore.
Oh Bobo was ready, but the fire chief said "Not!"
"A dragon can't be what a dragon is not."

So poor Bobo moped, feeling that he would never
Get to be Bobo the best fireman ever.
'Till there came one day a humungous fire turning
Clear up to the town, the whole forest to burning
The firemen fought. They were brave; took their lickins,
But the fire burned and burned. Oh, it burned like the dickens
And if it burned on, the whole town would be toast,
But it never happened. Though it happened—almost.
For Bobo, brave Bobo, to the fire he flew,
Shooting flames from his mouth, and his nostrils too,
Burned a wide path round the fire—and so
When the fire got there, there was no place to go.
So on that path the fire died.
And people laughed and people cried.
And Bobo said to everyone's delight,
"Sometimes you've just got to fight fire with fire,"
And you know—he was right!

In front of the firehouse and next to the street
Is a very large statue one's likely to meet
Of a very large creature on the fire wagon
That says *Bobo, Hero, and firefighting dragon,*
Who proved to us all—child, woman, and man—
That you can if you want to; if you want to you can.

Machu Picchu—pronounced Mah-Choo Pee-Choo—once a city occupied by the Inca Indians, sits eight thousand feet above sea level on a mountain rising from the floor of the Urubamba Valley in Peru. The Incas were an advanced civilization that practiced human sacrifice and even the name of their city had a fascination to me. For the child, whose every step is an adventure, I wrote a rhythmic, tongue-twister, fantasy travelogue, in poetry, thinking its words and images might excite the young child to the wonders of travel.

Machu Picchu Choo-Choo

A five-year-old boy is sitting on his grampa's lap. Grampa is about to read him a book. The book's title is The Machu Picchu Choo-choo.

Chico, Chico, I can teach-choo
How to get to Machu Picchu
On a train that's gonna scoot-choo.
It's the Machu Picchu Choo-choo.

Board a train of stones and sticks,
Rocks and clay, grass and bricks,
Squeaks and creeks and clacks and clicks,
Lizards, llamas, goats, and chicks.

To the click-clack and the clatter
You can hear the chomp and chatter
Of muchachas and muchachos
Munching Machu Picchu Nachos.

There is something to delight-choo,
Herky-jerky monkeys sight-choo,
Spunky monkeys in the trees
They Hokey Pokey just to please.

Choo-choo up past palms and pines
Toward pinnacles and granite shrines.
Listen to the caws and coos
Of cockatiels and cockatoos.

Choo-choo chugs and spurts and sputters,
Yanks and clanks and shakes and shudders,
Leaps and lurches, plunges, pitches,
Sways and totters, tugs and twitches.

When it gets up to the top
It grinds and screeches to a stop.
You're up so high no cloud can reach-choo.
You have come to Machu Picchu!

Machu Picchu, Machu Picchu!
Not an Inca there to greet-choo.
Secrets sleep within its stones,
And mummy's tombs and buried bones.

Buy a Machu Picchu flute to
Toot-toot, toot-toot, toot-toot, toot-choo
When you go back to your home
Aboard the Machu Picchu Choo-choo.

Hop atop a llama poppa!
Listen to the clippa-cloppa
As you ride the Inca trail
Above the forest's greenish veil.

Walk the mountains taking care
To view the heavens; breathe the air.
For once the magic casts its spell
You'll never ever say farewell.

When your trip has reached its end,
I bet-choo make that trip again.
Every sight and sound will suit-choo
On that Machu Picchu Choo-choo.

Grampa has fallen asleep on the chair. Chico is sleeping on his lap. The book has fallen to the floor. In Chico's arms lies a flute. On the flute, in bold letters, it says **Made in Machu Picchu.**

To consider the potential of a child, one has only to imagine his possibilities. The operative word here is *imagine*, for it's imagination, to a large extent, that determines what becomes of us. Before the child sets out to do something, or to become someone, he must first imagine that it's possible. Thus, imagination underlies accomplishment and nourishes creativity.

The following is an unpublished short story I wrote, initially intended for children, entitled "There's a Fantazzly in Your Noodle." "Fantazzly" is a play on the words *silly fantasy*, which stand for imagination.

The story shows how each and every one of us has an imagination and how it can, in turn, help us find life more interesting and fun.

There's a Fantazzly in Your Noodle

Cecil's bored. "What am I going to do today? There's no one to play with. Grampa's hammering on the side of the house. He won't play with me. He's too busy. Baby sister's in the buggy. She can't play with me. She's too little. Those older boys won't play with me. They're too big." (The older boys are flying kites and playing baseball in the field.) "I hate vacations, there's nothing to do."

"Nothing to do?" Cecil hears a tiny voice behind him. "Are you bonkers? Gaga? Got some screws loose? There's always something to do."

Cecil turns around to see who's talking, but he sees nothing. "I am here. Over here," says the voice. The voice belongs to a peculiar creature standing on his shoulder. It's two inches tall, skinny as a straw, with a big head on one end and tiny feet on the other. His hair sits on top his head like an eagle's nest, and his eyes bulge like purple walnuts above a long narrow nose.

"Oh my," Cecil says. "Who are you?"

"Who am I? Who am I? I'm your fantazzly," the creature answers. "And don't say you don't know what a fantazzly is."

"What is a fantazzly anyhow?"

"A fantazzly's an imagination. Everyone's got one."

"But where do you come from? I've never seen you before."

"Where do I come from? Why everywhere. And wherever. Wherever you are, that is. That's where I come from. I'm always with you. Inside your noodle."

"I have a fantazzly inside my noodle?"

"You betcha."

"What's my noodle?"

"Your noodle? Why it's your noggin. Your head."

"I have a fantazzly inside my head?"

"That's me. I'm your imagination, and I go with you wherever you go. I talk to you and help you see things you never saw before. For instance, look at that sky."

"What for? I've seen it before. It's just a sky."

"Just a sky? Just a sky? Use your peepers, you'll see it's not just a sky. Look again. See? It's full of marshmallows."

The fantazzly, now standing on its head in the grass, says, "I can help you see with your eyes closed. I can help you dream with your eyes open. When there's nothing to hear, I whisper in your ear."

"Whatcha standing on your head for?" asks Cecil.

"What for? What for? Why, anyone with a fantazzly knows what for. To see green rain, that's what for. And you could too."

Cecil tries it. "Wow!"

"Look at your baby sister," says the fantazzly. "Between those covers she looks like a hotdog." Cecil chuckles.

"And listen to that plane. It sounds like a roaring skyfish."

Cecil looks up at the kites in the sky. "And they look like swooping sail birds," he says.

"Now you're getting it," says the fantazzly.

The sky suddenly turns dark as if a smokey shade is being pulled over their heads and under the sky. The wind starts blowing. Dandelion fluffs whiz by. "Watch out for those fuzzy white spiders," the fantazzly says.

On the baseball field a gust of wind blows the players' caps off their heads. "Flying pots," Cecil says with glee.

Suddenly, it starts to rain. Rain streaks down Cecil's face. His clothes are soaked and soggy and dripping and drooping. Cecil says, "Look at me. I'm a candle, and I'm melting."

"Oh no, you're not a candle," says the fantazzly. "You're an ice cream cone. Cecil and the fantazzly find this very funny.

Then, as quickly as it starts, the rain stops. The sun comes out, and a rainbow appears in the sky. "The sky is smiling," says the fantazzly.

The sun begins to drop in the sky. Cecil and his fantazzly sit by a tree to watch the sunset.

"It looks like an orange-red balloon," says Cecil.

"The sun's getting tired and going to sleep," says the fantazzly.

Soon it's time for Cecil to go home. "Will you come home with me, fantazzly?"

"Home with you? Certainly. Naturally. Of course. Remember, I'm everywhere and wherever. Wherever you are, that is. That's where I am."

When it's time for bed, Cecil looks up and out his window. Stars sparkle and shoot through the night sky. "I know what to call the sky," says Cecil, "I'll call it the 'firefly hotel.'"

Cecil closes his eyes and goes to sleep. He can hardly wait for the morning so he can play with his fantazzly.

His fantazzly, standing on the bedpost, winks.

What's Wrong with Hannibal?

Hannibal was a lion.

"What's wrong with Hannibal?" asked Father. "He reads too much."

"He's got brains," said Mother. "He might as well use 'em."

Spike wanted to fight Hannibal, but Hannibal wouldn't fight.

"'C'mon and fight, you big pussycat," said Spike.

"What's wrong with Hannibal?" asked Father. "Whoever heard of a lion that won't fight?"

"He doesn't believe in violence. He's a pacifist," said Mother.

"*What kind of lion is that?*" wondered Father.

While everyone in Hannibal's family ate leg of lamb, Hannibal ate vegetables.

"You don't like my cooking, Hannibal?" asked Mother.

"Pass the broccoli," said Hannibal.

"Hannibal's one weird cat," Father told Mother.

Mother replied, "Hannibal's **one of a kind**, that's all. He marches to the beat of a different drummer."

"*I still think he's weird,*" thought Father.

While other lions fought, Hannibal read books.

"What's wrong with Hannibal?" asked his Father. "Why isn't he out fighting like the others his age?"

Hannibal painted. And liked gentle music.

Father worried he would never amount to anything. But Mother said,

"Don't worry about Hannibal, dear, he's just not **mainstream**. He's got brains. He might as well use them."

"*He's got teeth and claws too,*" thought Father. But he said nothing.

Hannibal announced he was going to college.

While other students partied, Hannibal studied. Hannibal joined the debate team. He became the school's star debater.

When Hannibal went home for the holidays, he was different.

"It's a real jungle out there," said Hannibal.

"*Of course,*" thought Father. "*What does he expect?*"

Hannibal graduated **summa cum lion**, which was the honor the school gave him for being first in his class. He gave the best speech his parents ever heard. Of course, it was the only speech they ever heard as well.

Hannibal returned to the plains where he spoke to the animals about education, conflict resolution, and taking care of each other and the grass.

All the animals of the plains respected Hannibal, and he was elected president of the plains—for life!

Mother was very proud of her one-of-a-kind son, and Father never asked what's wrong with Hannibal again.

How Do You Do It, Doc?

"How do you do it, Doc?" I can't imagine how many times I've been asked that question. I hear it on days the phone is ringing off the wall, when pages from the front desk are relentless, and when every room is filled with a screaming "mini." I hear it when a patient's resistance to examination borders on the violent, and I hear it when a problem has roused me from bed and required a trip to a home or hospital at three o'clock in the morning. And I ask myself that same question when I go to the office, day after day, with sniffles and headache or fever, which I undoubtedly picked up from one of the little patients.

One day a parent called our office so upset his child was still coughing.[7] He stated he was going to come into our office

---

[7] Apparently, the father had brought his son to our office a number of times for a chronic cough. Some combination of worry, frustration, and rage led him to make the threat. The police were called, and the father was told he could no longer bring his child to the office. Unfortunately, although the father later called to apologize and appeared truly repentant, we suggested he transfer his child to another office, for we could not comfortably see the child again.

with his gun and blow our brains out. For some time after that, I had a pervasive sense of unease returning to work. (At that time, I didn't ask myself, "**How** do you do it, Doc?" I asked myself, "**Why** do you do it, Doc?"

"How do you do it, Doc?" It's a good question—especially to one who's been hit, bit, scratched, kicked, spit at, peed on, and sued as well, all in the course of a day's work.

"How do you do it, Doc?" In thirty-five years of pediatric practice, one accumulates his or her share of worries, tears, abuse, and aggravation—always with that nagging fear of having made that one dreaded mistake in the course of one thousand decisions in a single day.

So if it was so bad, why did I keep doing it? With an undergraduate degree in literature, I could always have joined the ranks of the unemployed and become a philosopher. With my passion for art, I could certainly have decided on a career as a full-time artist (and refined the fine art of starvation).

Despite the negatives (after all there are those in every job), there was always much more than enough to keep me going, to make me happy.

I never regretted for a moment my choice to be a pediatrician. I always felt lucky to have found an occupation where my abilities and interests matched the job requirements. I have always enjoyed contact with people, and pediatrics certainly allowed that. Daily contact with kids helped keep me young and optimistic, and provided enduring friendships. The work has given me more than ample opportunity to express my creativity and to exercise a sense of humor. I've been able to prevent disease and to treat illness, as well as to aid in molding the development of children. I feel most fortunate to have chosen a profession that's provided me stroking, status, and income. And finally, I can think of nothing I could have done that would have given me a greater feeling of meaningful accomplishment.

When I'm asked, "How do you do it, Doc?" I usually smile, shrug my shoulders as if to say, "*It might be better than you think,*" and continue working. But that's the short form. For those who've asked and been dissatisfied with my answer, I only hope they go out and buy then read this book.

.

More Pictures

Look up in the sky. It's a bird.

No, It's a plane. No It's Superman!

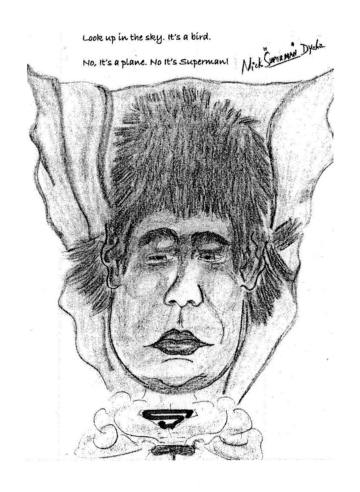

Michael Plevys
" ANGEL WITH HORN
11-14-91

Marissa
"I love Bandaids"
Ofewlock.

9-3-94

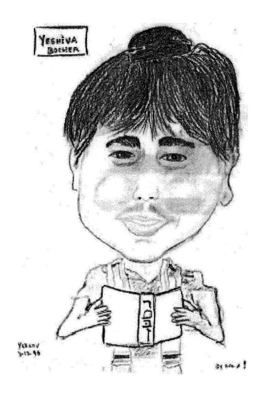

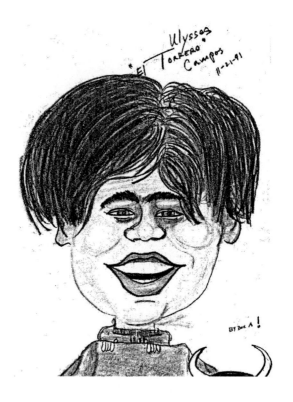

Book Summary

That's My Belly Button is a book of memoirs that finds its voice in both serious and humorous anecdotes, conversations, case histories, personal views, serendipitous events, and caricatures of patients treated in the office and hospital over a period of thirty-five years. The book creates a unique view of childhood and pediatrics as seen by the pediatrician—from the inside out.

Author's Biography

Neil Aronson lives with his wife, Evelyn, in Skokie, Illinois, on the outskirts of Chicago in an "empty nest" full of many books, telephone jacks, dragons, original art, and unfinished projects. He has two daughters who attended Niles North High School and, later, the University of Michigan. Dr. Aronson started writing children's books out of a desire to introduce children to fine art and fine artists, to stimulate their imaginations, and to excite them to the idea of travel and adventure—as well as to help them to deal with important aspects of growth and development, such as emerging independence and positive self-image. He's had an ample opportunity to watch and help kids grow, play, and interact in his past thirty-four years of work as a pediatrician. His office is filled with caricatures of the many children he's cared for, which he has been able to draw—usually in a few minutes—when time permitted. He has written all of his life and is currently refining a book and lyrics to what he hopes will be a finished musical soon. "My only regret as far as this book is concerned," states Dr. Aronson, "has to do with the lapses during which I saw patients but failed to record the interesting or humorous experiences in my journal and which are long since forgotten."